Contents

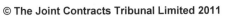

258   833

Schedules

Articles of Agreement

This Agreement is made the _____ 20 _____

Between   **The Employer** _____

_____

_____ (Company No._____)[1]

of/whose registered office is at _____

_____

_____

And   **The Contractor** _____

_____

_____ (Company No. _____)[1]

of/whose registered office is at _____

_____

_____

---

[1]   Where the Employer or Contractor is neither a company incorporated under the Companies Acts nor a company registered under the laws of another country, delete the references to Company number and registered office. In the case of a company incorporated outside England and Wales, particulars of its place of incorporation should be inserted immediately before its Company number. As to execution by foreign companies and matters of jurisdiction, see the Intermediate Building Contract Guide.

Recitals

Whereas

First   the Employer wishes to have the following work carried out[2]:

_____

_____

at _____

_____ ('the Works')
and has had drawings and bills of quantities or a specification or work schedules prepared which
show and describe the work to be done;

Second   the drawings are numbered/listed in _____

_____ annexed to this Contract
('the Contract Drawings') and have for identification been signed or initialled by or on behalf of
each Party[3];

Third   the Employer has supplied to the Contractor:

the Bills of Quantities[4]

the Specification[4]

the Work Schedules[4]

particulars of the Intermediate Named Sub-Contract Tender & Agreement ICSub/NAM
(comprising a certified copy of the tender for work included in the Bills of Quantities,
Specification or Work Schedules for pricing by the Contractor and for which the Contractor is
required under clause 3·7 to employ a named person, together with the Intermediate Named
Sub-Contract Invitation to Tender and Tender (ICSub/NAM/IT and ICSub/NAM/T) as
completed and the Tender Documents referred to in them)[5];

Fourth   the Contractor has:

(A)   priced the Bills of Quantities/Specification/Work Schedules[4] (as priced, 'the Priced
Document'), the total of such pricing being the Contract Sum stated in Article 2 ('Pricing
Option A'); or

---

[2]   State nature and location of intended works.

[3]   State the identifying numbers of the Contract Drawings or identify the schedule of drawings or other document listing them, which
should be annexed to this Contract, and make the appropriate deletions. The drawings themselves should be signed or initialled by or
on behalf of each Party.

[4]   Delete as appropriate.

[5]   Delete if no items specifying a Named Sub-Contractor are included in the documents. See the Intermediate Building Contract Guide.

(B)   stated the sum he will require for carrying out the Works shown on the Contract Drawings and described in the Specification, that sum being the Contract Sum stated in Article 2, and has supplied to the Employer a Contract Sum Analysis in accordance with the stated requirements of the Employer or a Schedule of Rates on which that sum is based ('the Priced Document') ('Pricing Option B');

and has provided the Employer with the priced schedule of activities annexed to this Contract ('the Activity Schedule')[6];

the Priced Document, the priced Activity Schedule, where provided, and (where Pricing Option B applies) the (unpriced) Specification have each for identification been signed or initialled by or on behalf of each Party;

Fifth   for the purposes of the Construction Industry Scheme (CIS) under the Finance Act 2004, the status of the Employer is, as at the Base Date, that stated in the Contract Particulars;

Sixth   the Employer has provided the Contractor with a schedule ('the Information Release Schedule') which states the information the Architect/Contract Administrator will release and the time of that release[7];

Seventh   for the purposes of the Construction (Design and Management) Regulations 2007 (the 'CDM Regulations') the status of the project that comprises or includes the Works is stated in the Contract Particulars;

Eighth   the division of the Works into Sections is shown in the Bills of Quantities/Specification/Work Schedules and/or the Contract Drawings or in such other documents as are identified in the Contract Particulars[8];

Ninth   where so stated in the Contract Particulars, this Contract is supplemented by the Framework Agreement identified in those particulars;

Tenth   the Supplemental Provisions identified in the Contract Particulars apply;

---

[6]   Delete these lines if a priced Activity Schedule is not provided.
In the Activity Schedule, each activity should be priced, so that the sum of those prices equals the Contract Sum excluding Provisional Sums and the value of work for which Approximate Quantities are included in the priced Bills of Quantities.

[7]   Delete the Sixth Recital if an Information Release Schedule is not provided.

[8]   Delete the Eighth Recital if the Works are not divided into Sections.

Now it is hereby agreed as follows

Article 1: Contractor's obligations

The Contractor shall carry out and complete the Works in accordance with the Contract Documents.

Article 2: Contract Sum

The Employer shall pay the Contractor at the times and in the manner specified in the Conditions the VAT-exclusive sum of

_____

_____ (£_____ . _____)('the Contract Sum')

or such other sum as shall become payable under this Contract.

Article 3: Architect/Contract Administrator

For the purposes of this Contract the Architect/Contract Administrator is

_____

of _____

_____

or, if he ceases to be the Architect/Contract Administrator, such other person as the Employer shall nominate in accordance with clause 3·4 of the Conditions.

Article 4: Quantity Surveyor

For the purposes of this Contract the Quantity Surveyor[9] is

_____

of _____

_____

or, if he ceases to be the Quantity Surveyor, such other person as the Employer shall nominate in accordance with clause 3·4 of the Conditions.

---

[9]   If the Architect/Contract Administrator is to exercise the Quantity Surveyor's functions under the Conditions, his name should be inserted in Article 4.

Article 5: CDM Co-ordinator

The CDM Co-ordinator for the purposes of the CDM Regulations is the Architect/Contract Administrator

(or)[10] _____

of _____

_____

or, if he ceases to be the CDM Co-ordinator, such other person as the Employer shall appoint pursuant to regulation 14(3) of those regulations.

Article 6: Principal Contractor

The Principal Contractor for the purposes of the CDM Regulations and the SWMP Regulations is the Contractor

(or)[10] _____

of _____

_____

or, if he ceases to be the Principal Contractor, such other contractor as the Employer shall appoint pursuant to regulation 14(3) of the CDM Regulations and/or regulation 4 of the SWMP Regulations.

Article 7: Adjudication

If any dispute or difference arises under this Contract, either Party may refer it to adjudication in accordance with clause 9·2.[11]

Article 8: Arbitration

Where Article 8 applies[12], then, subject to Article 7 and the exceptions set out below, any dispute or difference between the Parties of any kind whatsoever arising out of or in connection with this Contract shall be referred to arbitration in accordance with clauses 9·3 to 9·8 and the JCT 2011 edition of the Construction Industry Model Arbitration Rules (CIMAR). The exceptions to this Article 8 are:

- any disputes or differences arising under or in respect of the Construction Industry Scheme or VAT, to the extent that legislation provides another method of resolving such disputes or differences; and

- any disputes or differences in connection with the enforcement of any decision of an Adjudicator.

---

[10] Insert the name of the CDM Co-ordinator only where the Architect/Contract Administrator is not to fulfil that role, and that of the Principal Contractor only if that is to be a person other than the Contractor. If the project that comprises or includes the Works is not notifiable under the CDM Regulations 2007 – see the Contract Particulars (Seventh Recital), delete Articles 5 and 6 in their entirety.

[11] As to adjudication in cases where the Employer is a residential occupier within the meaning of section 106 of the Housing Grants, Construction and Regeneration Act 1996, see the Intermediate Building Contract Guide.

[12] If it is intended, subject to the right of adjudication and exceptions stated in Article 8, that disputes or differences should be determined by arbitration and not by legal proceedings, the Contract Particulars **must** state that Article 8 and clauses 9·3 to 9·8 apply and the words "do not apply" **must** be deleted. If the Parties wish any dispute or difference to be determined by the courts of another jurisdiction the appropriate amendment should be made to Article 9 (see also clause 1·11).

Article 9: Legal proceedings[12]

Subject to Article 7 and (where it applies) to Article 8, the English courts shall have jurisdiction over any dispute or difference between the Parties which arises out of or in connection with this Contract.

*Note: An asterisk * indicates text that is to be deleted as appropriate.*

Part 1: General

Clause etc.	*Subject*	
Fifth Recital and clause 4·5	Construction Industry Scheme (CIS)	Employer at the Base Date * is a 'contractor'/is not a 'contractor' for the purposes of the CIS
Seventh Recital	CDM Regulations[13]	the project * is/is not notifiable
Eighth Recital	Description of Sections (if any) *(If not shown or described in the Bills of Quantities/Specification/Work Schedules or the Contract Drawings, state the reference numbers and dates or other identifiers of documents in which they are shown.)*[14]	_____ _____ _____ _____
Ninth Recital	Framework Agreement (if applicable) *(State date, title and parties.)*	_____ _____ _____ _____
Tenth Recital and Schedule 5	Supplemental Provisions *(Where neither entry against an item below is deleted, the relevant paragraph applies.)*	
	Collaborative working	Paragraph 1 * applies/does not apply
	Health and safety	Paragraph 2 * applies/does not apply
	Cost savings and value improvements	Paragraph 3 * applies/does not apply
	Sustainable development and environmental considerations	Paragraph 4 * applies/does not apply

---

[13] A project is not notifiable under the CDM Regulations where it is not likely to involve more than 30 days, or 500 person days, of construction work or it is being carried out for a homeowner as a purely domestic project.

[14] If the relevant document or set of documents takes the form of an Annex to this Contract, it is sufficient to refer to that Annex.

Performance Indicators and monitoring		Paragraph 5 * applies/does not apply
Notification and negotiation of disputes		Paragraph 6 * applies/does not apply
Where paragraph 6 applies, the respective nominees of the Parties are		Employer's nominee

_____

_____

Contractor's nominee

_____

_____

or such replacement as each Party may notify to the other from time to time

Article 8	Arbitration *(If neither entry is deleted, Article 8 and clauses 9·3 to 9·8 do not apply. If disputes and differences are to be determined by arbitration and not by legal proceedings, it <u>must</u> be stated that Article 8 and clauses 9·3 to 9·8 apply.)*[15]	Article 8 and clauses 9·3 to 9·8 (*Arbitration*) * apply/do not apply
1·1	Base Date	_____
1·1	CDM Planning Period[16]	shall mean the period of _____ * days/weeks * ending on the Date of Possession/ * beginning/ending on _____ 20 _____
1·1	Date for Completion of the Works *(where completion by Sections does not apply)*	_____
	Sections: Dates for Completion of Sections[17]	Section _____ : _____ Section _____ : _____ Section _____ : _____

---

[15]   On factors to be taken into account by the Parties in considering whether disputes are to be determined by arbitration or by legal proceedings, see the Intermediate Building Contract Guide. See also footnote [12].

[16]   Under the CDM Regulations 2007 every client is expressly required to allocate sufficient time (the CDM Planning Period) prior to the commencement of construction to enable contractors and others to carry out necessary CDM planning and preparation. There may be cases where that planning and preparation needs to be completed earlier than the Date of Possession and adaptation of the entries may be needed where there are Sections.

[17]   Continue on further sheets if necessary, which should be signed or initialled by or on behalf of each Party and then be annexed to this Contract.

1·7	Addresses for service of notices by the Parties *(If none is stated, the address in each case, subject to clause 1·7·3, shall be that shown at the commencement of the Agreement.)*[18]	Employer _____
		_____
		_____
		Contractor _____
		_____
		_____

2·4	Date of Possession of the site *(where possession by Sections does not apply)*	_____ 20____
	Sections: Dates of Possession of Sections[17]	Section ____ : _____ 20____
		Section ____ : _____ 20____
		Section ____ : _____ 20____

2·5	Deferment of possession of the site *(where possession by Sections does not apply)*	Clause 2·5 * applies/does not apply Maximum period of deferment (if less than 6 weeks) is _____
	Sections: deferment of possession of Sections	Clause 2·5 * applies/does not apply Maximum period of deferment (if less than 6 weeks) is[17] Section ____ : _____ Section ____ : _____ Section ____ : _____

2·23·2	Liquidated damages *(where completion by Sections does not apply)*	at the rate of £ _____ per _____
	Sections: rate of liquidated damages for each Section[17]	Section ____ : £ _____ per _____ Section ____ : £ _____ per _____ Section ____ : £ _____ per _____

2·29	Sections: Section Sums[17]	Section ____ : £ _____ Section ____ : £ _____ Section ____ : £ _____

---

[18]   As to service of notices etc. outside the United Kingdom, see the Intermediate Building Contract Guide.

2·30	Rectification Period *(where completion by Sections does not apply)* *(If no other period is stated, the period is 6 months.)*	_____ months from the date of practical completion of the Works

Sections: Rectification Periods[17]
(If no other period is stated, the period is 6 months.)

Section _____ : _____ months

Section _____ : _____ months

Section _____ : _____ months
from the date of practical completion of each Section

4·6   Advance payment
(Not applicable where the Employer is a Local Authority)

*   Clause 4·6
applies/does not apply

If applicable:
the advance payment will be[19]

£ _____ /

_____ per cent of the Contract Sum

and will be paid to the Contractor on

_____ ;

it will be reimbursed to the Employer in the following amount(s) and at the following time(s)

_____

_____

_____

_____

4·6   Advance Payment Bond
(Not applicable where the Employer is a Local Authority)
(Where an advance payment is to be made, an advance payment bond is required unless stated that it is not required.)

*   An advance payment bond
is/is not required

4·7·1   Interim payments – due dates
(If no date is stated, the first due date is one month after the Date of Possession.)

The first due date is:

_____

and thereafter the same date in each month or the nearest Business Day in that month[20]

---

[19]   Insert either a monetary amount or a percentage figure, delete the alternative and complete the other required details.

[20]   The first date should not be more than one month after the Date of Possession. Where it is intended that interim payments should become due on the last day of each month, the entry may be completed/amended to read "the last day of *(insert month)* and thereafter the last day in each month or the nearest Business Day in that month." After practical completion, clause 4·7·1·3 allows for intervals of 2 months (or such other period as the Parties agree) between interim payments.

4·8·1	Interim payments – percentages of value	
	Where the Works, or those works in a Section, have not achieved practical completion, the percentage of total value in respect of the works that have not achieved practical completion is *(The percentage is 95 per cent unless a different rate is stated.)*	_____ per cent[21]
	Where the Works, or those works in a Section, have achieved practical completion, the percentage in respect of the completed works is *(The percentage is 97½ per cent unless a different rate is stated.)*	_____ per cent[21]
4·9·4	Listed Items – uniquely identified *(Delete the entry if no bond is required.)*	* For uniquely identified Listed Items a bond in respect of payment for such items is required for £ _____
4·9·5	Listed Items – not uniquely identified *(Delete the entry if clause 4·9·5 does not apply.)*	* For Listed Items that are not uniquely identified a bond in respect of payment for such items is required for £ _____
4·15 and Schedule 4	Contribution, levy and tax fluctuations	Schedule 4 *(Fluctuations Option)* applies[22]
	Percentage addition for Fluctuations Option, paragraph 12	_____ per cent
6·4·1·2	Contractor's insurance: injury to persons or property – insurance cover *(for any one occurrence or series of occurrences arising out of one event)*	£ _____
6·5·1	Insurance – liability of Employer *(Not required unless it is stated that it may be required and the minimum amount of indemnity is stated)*	Insurance * may be required/is not required Minimum amount of indemnity for any one occurrence or series of occurrences arising out of one event £ _____ [23]

---

[21]   An insertion is needed here only if the default position is not to apply. If no retention is required, insert '100' in the entries for clause 4·8·1.

[22]   Delete if the contract period is of such limited duration as to make the provision inappropriate.

[23]   If the indemnity is to be for an aggregate amount and not for any one occurrence or series of occurrences the entry should be amended to make this clear.

6·7 and Schedule 1	Insurance of the Works – Insurance Options [24][25]	Schedule 1: * Insurance Option A applies/ * Insurance Option B applies/ * Insurance Option C applies
6·7 and Schedule 1 Insurance Option A (paragraphs A·1 and A·3), B (paragraph B·1) or C (paragraph C·2)	Percentage to cover professional fees *(If no other percentage is stated, it shall be 15 per cent.)*	_____ per cent
6·7 and Schedule 1 Insurance Option A (paragraph A·3)	Annual renewal date of insurance *(as supplied by the Contractor)*	_____
6·10 and Schedule 1	Terrorism Cover – details of the required cover *(State reference numbers and dates or other identifiers of documents setting out the requirements. Unless otherwise stated, Pool Re Cover is required.)*	_____ _____ _____ _____
6·12	Joint Fire Code	The Joint Fire Code * applies/does not apply[26]
	If the Joint Fire Code applies, state whether the insurer under Schedule 1, Insurance Option A, B or C (paragraph C·2) has specified that the Works are a 'Large Project':	* Yes/No [26]
6·15	Joint Fire Code – amendments/revisions *(The cost shall be borne by the Contractor unless otherwise stated.)*	The cost, if any, of compliance with amendment(s) or revision(s) to the Joint Fire Code shall be borne by * the Employer/the Contractor
8·9·2	Period of suspension *(If none is stated, the period is 2 months.)*	_____
8·11·1·1 to 8·11·1·5	Period of suspension *(If none is stated, the period is 2 months.)*	_____

---

[24] Delete all but one.

[25] Obtaining Terrorism Cover, which is necessary in order to comply with the requirements of Insurance Option A, B or C, will involve an additional premium and may in certain situations be difficult to effect. Where a difficulty arises discussion should take place between the Parties and their insurance advisers. See the Intermediate Building Contract Guide.

[26] Where Insurance Option A applies these entries are made on information supplied by the Contractor.

9·2·1	Adjudication[27]	The Adjudicator is _____
	Nominating body – where no Adjudicator is named or where the named Adjudicator is unwilling or unable to act (whenever that is established)[28] *(Where an Adjudicator is not named and a nominating body has not been selected, the nominating body shall be one of the bodies listed opposite selected by the Party requiring the reference to adjudication.)*	* Royal Institute of British Architects * The Royal Institution of Chartered Surveyors * constructionadjudicators.com[29] * Association of Independent Construction Adjudicators[30] * Chartered Institute of Arbitrators
9·4·1	Arbitration[31] – appointor of Arbitrator (and of any replacement)[32] *(If no appointor is selected, the appointor shall be the President or a Vice-President of the Royal Institute of British Architects.)*	President or a Vice-President: * Royal Institute of British Architects * The Royal Institution of Chartered Surveyors * Chartered Institute of Arbitrators

---

[27]   The Parties should either name the Adjudicator and select the nominating body or, alternatively, select only the nominating body. The Adjudication Agreement (Adj) and the Adjudication Agreement (Named Adjudicator) (Adj/N) have been prepared by JCT for use when appointing an Adjudicator.

[28]   Delete all but one of the nominating bodies asterisked.

[29]   constructionadjudicators.com is a trading name of Contractors Legal Grp Ltd.

[30]   Association of Independent Construction Adjudicators acts as an agent of and is controlled by the National Specialist Contractors' Council for the purpose of the nomination of adjudicators.

[31]   This only applies where the Contract Particulars state (against the reference to Article 8) that Article 8 and clauses 9·3 to 9·8 *(Arbitration)* apply.

[32]   Delete all but one of the bodies asterisked.

Part 2: Collateral Warranties

If collateral warranties are required from the Contractor, complete the particulars in (A) to (D) below:

Purchaser and Tenant Warranties

(A) Identity of Purchasers/Tenants in whose favour Collateral Warranties may be required

Clauses
7·4 and 7·6
of the Conditions

Name, class or description of person	The part of the Works to be purchased or let
_____	_____

(Where no Purchasers or Tenants are identified by name, class or description, no collateral warranties in favour of such persons shall be required from the Contractor.)

Clause of CWa/P&T	(B) Contractor's Warranties – Purchasers and Tenants	
1·1·2	Applicability of clause 1·1·2	Clause 1·1·2 * applies/does not apply
	Maximum liability *(Unless clause 1·1·2 is stated to apply and the maximum liability is stated, clause 1·1·2 does not apply.)*	The maximum liability is £ _____
	Type of maximum liability *(If not stated, it shall be an aggregate limit on liability.)*	* Maximum liability is in respect of each breach/ * Maximum liability is an aggregate limit on liability
1·3·1	Net Contribution: Consultants *(If none are specified, these shall be the Architect/Contract Administrator and the Quantity Surveyor (including any replacements), together with any other consultants who agree to give collateral warranties (or undertakings in similar terms) to any Purchaser(s) and/or Tenant(s).)*	For the purposes of clause 1·3·1 'the Consultants' are: _____ _____ _____ _____
1·3·2	Net Contribution: Sub-Contractors *(If none are specified, these shall be such as agree to give collateral warranties (or undertakings in similar terms) to any Purchaser(s) and/or Tenant(s).)*	For the purposes of clause 1·3·2 'the Sub-Contractors' are: _____ _____ _____ _____

Funder Warranties

Clauses 7·5 and 7·6 of the Conditions	(C) **Identity of Funder** *(If not identified by name, class or description, no warranty in favour of a Funder shall be required from the Contractor.)*	_____ _____
Clause of CWa/F	(D) **Contractor's Warranties – Funder**	
1·1	Net Contribution: Consultants and Sub-Contractors *(Unless otherwise stated, these shall be those specified (or deemed to be specified) under (B) above.)*	_____ _____

Collateral Warranties from Sub-Contractors

(E) If warranties are required from sub-contractors, complete the particulars below:

Clauses 3·5 and 3·6 of the Conditions	Sub-contractors from whom Warranties may be required[33]	Type(s) of warranty (SCWa/P&T, SCWa/F, SCWa/E) required[34] from each sub-contractor
	_____	_____

For these purposes, unless otherwise stated:

(i) all Purchasers and Tenants identified at (A) above, any Funder identified at (C) above and the Employer shall be entitled to a warranty from a sub-contractor where the appropriate type is shown above as required from him;

(ii) if a maximum liability is specified under (B) above, that shall also apply in relation to all sub-contractors' Collateral Warranties unless a lower amount is specified;

(iii) "the Consultants" for sub-contractors' Collateral Warranties shall be those stated in (B) above.

---

[33] Employers should be selective in listing the sub-contractors (or categories of sub-contractor) from whom collateral warranties may be required. The list of sub-contractors should **not** include any Named Sub-Contractor since such matters are intended to be dealt with by the Intermediate Named Sub-Contractor/Employer Agreement ICSub/NAM/E and not to be governed by the Intermediate Named Sub-Contract itself (ICSub/NAM). See the Intermediate Building Contract Guide.

[34] Where a sub-contractor is required to grant the Collateral Warranties of the types referred to in clause 7·6 (i.e. the Sub-Contractor Collateral Warranty for a Purchaser or Tenant (SCWa/P&T), for a Funder (SCWa/F) and for the Employer (SCWa/E)), state the particular type(s). All three Collateral Warranties are documents prepared by JCT.

Note on Execution

This Agreement should be executed by both the Employer and the Contractor either under hand or as a deed. As to factors relevant to that choice, see the Intermediate Building Contract Guide.

Execution under hand

If this Agreement is to be executed under hand, use the form set out on the following page. Each Party or his authorised representative should sign where indicated in the presence of a witness who should then sign and set out his name and address.

Execution as a Deed

If this Agreement is to be executed as a deed, each Party should use the relevant form marked 'Execution as a Deed' in accordance with the notes provided.

Other forms of Attestation

In cases where the forms of attestation set out are not appropriate, e.g. in the case of certain housing associations and partnerships or if a Party wishes an attorney to execute this Agreement on his behalf, the appropriate form(s) may be inserted in the vacant space opposite and/or below.

As witness

the hands of the Parties
or their duly authorised representatives

Signed by or on behalf of
the Employer

_____

in the presence of:

_____
witness' signature

_____
witness' name

_____
witness' address

_____

Signed by or on behalf of
the Contractor

_____

in the presence of:

_____
witness' signature

_____
witness' name

_____
witness' address

_____

Notes on Execution as a Deed

1   For the purposes of execution as a deed, two forms are provided for execution, one for the Employer and the other for the Contractor. Each form provides four methods of execution, **(A)** to **(D)**, for use as appropriate. The full name of the Employer or Contractor (whether an individual, a company or other body) should be inserted where indicated at the commencement of the relevant form. This applies irrespective of the method used.

2   For public and private companies incorporated and registered under the Companies Acts, the three principal methods of execution as a deed are:

(A) through signature by a Director and the Company Secretary or by two Directors;

(B) by affixing the company's common seal in the presence of a Director and the *Company* Secretary or of two Directors or other duly authorised officers; or

(C) signature by a single Director in the presence of a witness who attests the signature.

Methods **(A)** and **(C)** are available to public and private companies whether or not they have a common seal. (Method **(C)** was introduced by section 44(2)(b) of the Companies Act 2006.) Methods **(A)** and **(C)** are not available under companies legislation to local authorities or to certain other bodies corporate, e.g. bodies incorporated by letters patent or private Act of Parliament that are not registered under companies legislation and such bodies may only use method **(B)**.

3   Where method **(A)** is being used, delete the inappropriate words and insert in the spaces indicated the names of the two Directors, or of the Director and the Company Secretary, who are to sign.

4   If method **(B)** (affixing the common seal) is adopted in cases where either or both the authorised officers attesting its affixation are not themselves a Director or the *Company* Secretary, their respective office(s) should be substituted for the reference(s) to Director and/or to *Company* Secretary/Director. (In the case of execution by bodies that are not companies, the reference to "*Company*" under the second signature should be deleted where appropriate.)

5   Method **(C)** (execution by a single Director) has been introduced primarily, but not exclusively, for 'single officer' companies. The Director should sign where indicated in the presence of a witness who should then sign and set out his name and address.

6   Where the Employer or Contractor is an individual, he should use method **(D)** and sign where indicated in the presence of a witness who should then sign and set out his name and address.

Executed as a Deed by the Employer

namely [1] _____

(A) acting by a Director and the Company Secretary/two Directors **of the company** [2, 3]

_____   and   _____
(Print name of signatory)   *(Print name of signatory)*

_____   _____
Signature   Director   *Signature*   Company Secretary/Director

(B) by affixing hereto the common seal **of the company/other body corporate** [2, 4]

in the presence of

_____
Signature   Director

_____
Signature   Company Secretary/Director

[Common seal of company]

(C) by attested signature of a single Director **of the company** [2, 5]

_____
Signature   Director

in the presence of

Witness' signature _____ *(Print name)* _____

Witness' address _____

(D) by attested signature **of the individual** [6]

_____
Signature

in the presence of

Witness' signature _____ *(Print name)* _____

Witness' address _____

Note: The numbers on this page refer to the numbered paragraphs in the Notes on Execution as a Deed.

Executed as a Deed by the Contractor

namely [1] _____

(A) acting by a Director and the Company Secretary/two Directors **of the company** [2, 3]

_____   and   _____
(Print name of signatory)   *(Print name of signatory)*

_____   _____
Signature   Director   *Signature*   Company Secretary/Director

(B) by affixing hereto the common seal **of the company/other body corporate** [2, 4]

in the presence of

_____
Signature   Director

_____
Signature   Company Secretary/Director

[Common seal of company]

(C) by attested signature of a single Director **of the company** [2, 5]

_____
Signature   Director

in the presence of

Witness' signature _____ *(Print name)* _____

Witness' address _____

(D) by attested signature **of the individual** [6]

_____
Signature

in the presence of

Witness' signature _____ *(Print name)* _____

Witness' address _____

Note: The numbers on this page refer to the numbered paragraphs in the Notes on Execution as a Deed.

Conditions

Section 1   Definitions and Interpretation

Definitions

1·1   Unless the context otherwise requires or the Agreement or these Conditions specifically provide otherwise, the following words and phrases, where they appear in capitalised form in the Agreement or these Conditions, shall have the meanings stated or referred to below:

Word or phrase	Meaning
Activity Schedule:	see the **Fourth Recital**.
Adjudicator:	an individual appointed under **clause 9·2** as the Adjudicator.
Agreement:	the Articles of Agreement to which these Conditions are annexed, consisting of the Recitals, the Articles and the Contract Particulars.
All Risks Insurance:	see **clause 6·8**.
Approximate Quantity:	a quantity in any Contract Bills there identified as an approximate quantity.
Arbitrator:	an individual appointed under **clause 9·4** as the Arbitrator.
Architect/Contract Administrator:	the person named in **Article 3** or any successor nominated or otherwise agreed under **clause 3·4**.
Article:	an article in the **Agreement**.
Base Date:	the date stated as such in the **Contract Particulars** (against the reference to **clause 1·1**)[35].
Business Day:	any day which is not a Saturday, a Sunday or a Public Holiday.
CDM Co-ordinator:	the Architect/Contract Administrator or other person named in **Article 5** or any successor appointed by the Employer.
CDM Planning Period:	the minimum amount of time referred to in regulation 10(2)(c) of the CDM Regulations, as specified in the **Contract Particulars** (against the reference to **clause 1·1**).
CDM Regulations:	the Construction (Design and Management) Regulations 2007.
Completion Date:	the Date for Completion of the Works or of a Section as stated in the **Contract Particulars** or such other date as is fixed under **clause 2·19**.
Conditions:	the clauses set out in sections 1 to 9 of these Conditions, together with and including the Schedules hereto.

---

[35]   The Base Date is relevant (inter alia) to the Fluctuations Option (Schedule 4) and it helps to determine the edition/issue and/or version of documents relevant to this Contract, e.g. the Standard Method of Measurement and definitions of the prime cost of daywork (clause 5·4).

continued 1·1

Construction Industry Scheme (or 'CIS'):	see the **Fifth Recital**.
Construction Phase Plan:	the plan prepared by the Principal Contractor, where the project is notifiable under the CDM Regulations and in order to comply with regulation 23, including any updates and revisions.
Contract Bills:	(where Pricing Option A applies and Bills of Quantities form the Priced Document) those bills as priced by the Contractor (see the **Third** and **Fourth Recitals**).
Contract Documents:	the Agreement, these Conditions and the Contract Drawings, together with:
	(where Pricing Option A applies) the Priced Document or (where Pricing Option B applies) the Specification; and
	any Invitation to Tender and Tender to and by a Named Sub-Contractor in forms ICSub/NAM/IT and ICSub/NAM/T as referred to in the Third Recital.
Contract Drawings:	the drawings referred to in the **Second Recital**.
Contract Particulars:	the particulars in the **Agreement** and there described as such, including the entries made by the Parties.
Contract Sum:	the sum stated in **Article 2**.
Contract Sum Analysis:	see the **Fourth Recital**.
Contractor:	the person named as Contractor in the **Agreement**.
Contractor's Persons:	the Contractor's employees and agents, all other persons employed or engaged on or in connection with the Works or any part of them and any other person properly on the site in connection therewith, excluding the Architect/Contract Administrator, the Quantity Surveyor, the Employer, Employer's Persons and any Statutory Undertaker.
Date for Completion:	the date stated as such date in the **Contract Particulars** (against the reference to **clause 1·1**) in relation to the Works or a Section.
Date of Possession:	the date stated as such date in the **Contract Particulars** (against the reference to **clause 2·4**) in relation to the Works or a Section.
Employer:	the person named as Employer in the **Agreement**.
Employer's Persons:	all persons employed, engaged or authorised by the Employer, excluding the Contractor, Contractor's Persons, the Architect/Contract Administrator, the Quantity Surveyor and any Statutory Undertaker.
Excepted Risks:	see **clause 6·8**.
Final Certificate:	see **clauses 1·9** and **4·14**.
Final Payment Notice:	see **clause 4·14·6**.
Finance Agreement:	the agreement between the Funder and the Employer for the provision of finance for the Works.
Fluctuations Option:	the provisions set out in **Schedule 4** (see **clause 4·15** and the **Contract Particulars**).
Funder:	the person named or otherwise sufficiently identified as such in or by Part 2 of the Contract Particulars.
Information Release Schedule:	the schedule referred to in the **Sixth Recital**.
Insolvent:	see **clause 8·1**.

continued 1·1

Insurance Options A, B and C:	the provisions relating to insurance of the Works and (where applicable) existing structures set out in **Schedule 1**.
Interest Rate:	a rate 5% per annum above the official dealing rate of the Bank of England current at the date that a payment due under this Contract becomes overdue.
Interim Application:	see **clause 4·10**.
Interim Certificate:	any of the certificates to which **clause 4·7·2** refers.
Interim Payment Notice:	see **clause 4·10·2**.
Joint Fire Code:	the Joint Code of Practice on the Protection from Fire of Construction Sites and Buildings Undergoing Renovation, published by the Construction Confederation and the Fire Protection Association, current at the Base Date.
Joint Names Policy:	see **clause 6·8**.
Listed Items:	materials, goods and/or items prefabricated for inclusion in the Works which are listed as such items by the Employer in a list supplied to the Contractor and annexed (where Pricing Option A applies) to the Priced Document or (where Pricing Option B applies) to the Specification.
Named Sub-Contract Conditions:	Intermediate Named Sub-Contract Conditions ICSub/NAM/C (as incorporated by reference in an Intermediate Named Sub-Contract Agreement ICSub/NAM/A).
Named Sub-Contractor:	see the **Third Recital** and **clause 3·7**.
Parties:	the Employer and the Contractor together.
Party:	either the Employer or the Contractor.
Pay Less Notice:	see **clauses 4·11·5** and **4·12·1**.
Practical Completion Certificate:	see **clause 2·21**.
Priced Document:	see the **Fourth Recital**.
Pricing Options A and B:	see the **Fourth Recital**.
Principal Contractor:	the Contractor or other contractor named in **Article 6** or any successor appointed by the Employer.
Provisional Sum:	where the Contract Documents include Contract Bills, includes a sum provided in such bills for work, whether or not identified as being for defined or undefined work within the meaning of General Rule 10 of the Standard Method of Measurement; and
	where the Contract Documents do not include Contract Bills, includes a sum provided for work that the Employer may or may not decide to have carried out, or which cannot be accurately specified in the Contract Documents.
Public Holiday:	Christmas Day, Good Friday or a day which under the Banking and Financial Dealings Act 1971 is a bank holiday.[36]

---

[36]   Amend as necessary if different Public Holidays are applicable.

continued 1·1

Purchaser:	any person named or otherwise sufficiently identified as such (whether by class or description) in or by Part 2 of the Contract Particulars to whom the Employer transfers or agrees to transfer his interest in all or part of the Works.
Quantity Surveyor:	the person named in **Article 4** or any successor nominated or otherwise agreed under **clause 3·4**.
Recitals:	the recitals in the **Agreement**.
Rectification Period:	the period stated as such period in the **Contract Particulars** (against the reference to **clause 2·30**) in relation to the Works or (where applicable) a Section.
Relevant Date:	see **clause 2·25**.
Relevant Event:	see **clause 2·20**.
Relevant Matter:	see **clause 4·18**.
Relevant Part:	see **clause 2·25**.
Schedule of Rates:	see the **Fourth Recital**.
Scheme:	Part 1 of the Schedule to The Scheme for Construction Contracts (England and Wales) Regulations 1998.
Sections:	(where applicable) the Sections into which the Works have been divided, as referred to in the **Eighth Recital** and the **Contract Particulars**.
Section Completion Certificate:	see **clause 2·21·2**.
Section Sum:	see **clause 2·29** and the **Contract Particulars**.
Site Materials:	all unfixed materials and goods delivered to and placed on or adjacent to the Works which are intended for incorporation therein.
Specification:	where applicable under Pricing Option A, the specification as priced and, where Pricing Option B applies, the unpriced specification. (See the **Third** and **Fourth Recitals**.)
Specified Perils:	see **clause 6·8**.
Standard Method of Measurement:	the Standard Method of Measurement of Building Works, 7th Edition, produced by The Royal Institution of Chartered Surveyors and the Construction Confederation, current, unless otherwise stated in the Contract Documents, at the Base Date (references in that publication to 'the Appendix' being read as references to the Contract Particulars).
Statutory Requirements:	any statute, statutory instrument, regulation, rule or order made under any statute or directive having the force of law which affects the Works or performance of any obligations under this Contract and any regulation or bye-law of any local authority or statutory undertaker which has any jurisdiction with regard to the Works or with whose systems the Works are, or are to be, connected.
Statutory Undertaker:	any local authority or statutory undertaker where executing work solely in pursuance of its statutory obligations, including any persons employed, engaged or authorised by it upon or in connection with that work.
SWMP Regulations:	the Site Waste Management Plans Regulations 2008.
Tenant:	any person named or otherwise sufficiently identified as such (whether by class or description) in or by Part 2 of the Contract Particulars to whom the Employer grants or agrees to grant a leasehold interest in all or part of the Works.

continued 1·1

Terrorism Cover:	see **clause 6·8**.
Valuation:	a valuation by the Quantity Surveyor in accordance with the Valuation Rules, pursuant to **clause 5·2**.
Valuation Rules:	see **clauses 5·3** to **5·6**.
Variation:	see **clause 5·1**.
VAT:	Value Added Tax.
Works:	the works briefly described in the **First Recital**, as more particularly shown, described or referred to in the Contract Documents, including any changes made to those works in accordance with this Contract.
Work Schedules:	where applicable under Pricing Option A, the work schedules as priced (see the **Third** and **Fourth Recitals**).

Interpretation

Reference to clauses etc.

1·2   Unless otherwise stated, a reference in the Agreement or in these Conditions to a clause or Schedule is to that clause in or Schedule to these Conditions and, unless the context otherwise requires, a reference in a Schedule to a paragraph is to that paragraph of that Schedule.

Agreement etc. to be read as a whole

1·3   The Agreement and these Conditions are to be read as a whole but nothing contained in the Contract Bills/Specification/Work Schedules, nor anything in any Framework Agreement, shall override or modify the Agreement or these Conditions.

Headings, references to persons, legislation etc.

1·4   In the Agreement and these Conditions, unless the context otherwise requires:

·1   the headings are included for convenience only and shall not affect the interpretation of this Contract;

·2   the singular includes the plural and vice versa;

·3   a gender includes any other gender;

·4   a reference to a 'person' includes any individual, firm, partnership, company and any other body corporate; and

·5   a reference to a statute, statutory instrument or other subordinate legislation ('legislation') is to such legislation as amended and in force from time to time, including any legislation which re-enacts or consolidates it, with or without modification, and including corresponding legislation in any other relevant part of the United Kingdom.

Reckoning periods of days

1·5   Where under this Contract an act is required to be done within a specified period of days after or from a specified date, the period shall begin immediately after that date. Where the period would include a day which is a Public Holiday that day shall be excluded.

Contracts (Rights of Third Parties) Act 1999

1·6   Notwithstanding any other provision of this Contract, nothing in this Contract confers or is intended to confer any right to enforce any of its terms on any person who is not a party to it.

Notices and other communications

1·7   ·1   Any notice or other communication between the Parties, or by or to the Architect/Contract Administrator or Quantity Surveyor, that is expressly referred to in the Agreement or these Conditions (including, without limitation, each application, approval, consent, confirmation, counter-notice, decision, instruction or other notification) shall be in writing.

·2   Subject to clause 1·7·4, each such notice or other communication and any documents to be supplied may or (where so required) shall be sent or transmitted by the means (electronic or otherwise) and in such format as the Parties from time to time agree in writing for the purposes of this Contract.[37]

·3   Subject to clauses 1·7·2 and 1·7·4, any notice, communication or document may be given or served by any effective means and shall be duly given or served if delivered by hand or sent by pre-paid post to:

.1   the recipient's address stated in the Contract Particulars, or to such other address as the recipient may from time to time notify to the sender; or

.2   if no such address is then current, the recipient's last known principal business address or (where a body corporate) its registered or principal office.

·4   Any notice expressly required by this Contract to be given in accordance with this clause 1·7·4 shall be delivered by hand or sent by Recorded Signed for or Special Delivery post. Where sent by post in that manner, it shall, subject to proof to the contrary, be deemed to have been received on the second Business Day after the date of posting.

·5   If in an emergency any communication is made orally with respect to health and safety, risk of damage to property or insurance matters, written confirmation of it shall be sent as soon thereafter as is reasonably practicable.

Issue of Architect/Contract Administrator's certificates

1·8   Each certificate to be issued by the Architect/Contract Administrator under these Conditions shall be issued to the Employer and the Contractor at the same time.

Effect of Final Certificate

1·9   ·1   Except as provided in clauses 1·9·2 and 1·9·3 (and save in respect of fraud), the Final Certificate shall be conclusive evidence:

.1   that where and to the extent that any of the particular qualities of any materials or goods or any particular standard of an item of workmanship was described expressly in the Contract Drawings or in the Contract Bills/Specification/Work Schedules, or in any instruction issued by the Architect/Contract Administrator under these Conditions or in any drawings or details issued by the Architect/Contract Administrator under clause 2·9 or 2·10, to be for the approval of the Architect/Contract Administrator, the particular quality or standard was to the reasonable satisfaction of the Architect/Contract Administrator, but the Final Certificate shall not be conclusive that they or any other materials or goods or workmanship comply with any other requirement or term of this Contract;

.2   that any necessary effect has been given to all the terms of this Contract that require additions to, adjustments of or deductions from the Contract Sum, save in regard to any accidental inclusion or exclusion of any item or any arithmetical error in any computation;

.3   that all and only such extensions of time, if any, as are due under clause 2·19 have been given; and

.4   that the reimbursement of direct loss and/or expense, if any, to the Contractor pursuant to clause 4·17 is in final settlement of all and any claims which the Contractor has or may have arising out of the occurrence of any of the Relevant Matters, whether such claim be for breach of contract, duty of care, statutory duty or otherwise.

---

[37]   The Parties should agree a communications protocol on or before entering into the Contract, or as soon thereafter as is practicable. See the Intermediate Building Contract Guide.

continued 1·9

 ·2   If adjudication, arbitration or other proceedings are commenced by either Party before or not later than 28 days after the Final Certificate has been issued, the Final Certificate shall be conclusive evidence as provided in clause 1·9·1 save only in respect of the matters to which those proceedings relate.

 ·3   In the case of a dispute or difference on which an Adjudicator gives his decision on a date after the date of issue of the Final Certificate, if either Party wishes to have that dispute or difference determined by arbitration or legal proceedings, that Party may commence arbitration or legal proceedings within 28 days of the date on which the Adjudicator gives his decision.

Effect of certificates other than Final Certificate

1·10   Save as stated in clause 1·9 no certificate of the Architect/Contract Administrator shall of itself be conclusive evidence that any works, any materials or goods to which the certificate relates are in accordance with this Contract.

Applicable law

1·11   This Contract shall be governed by and construed in accordance with the law of England.[38]

---

[38]   Where the Parties do not wish the law applicable to this Contract to be the law of England appropriate amendments should be made.

Contractor's Obligations

General obligations

2·1   The Contractor shall carry out and complete the Works in a proper and workmanlike manner and in compliance with the Contract Documents, the Construction Phase Plan (where applicable) and other Statutory Requirements, and shall give all notices required by the Statutory Requirements.

Materials, goods and workmanship

2·2   ·1   Where and to the extent that approval of the quality of materials or goods or of the standards of workmanship is a matter for the Architect/Contract Administrator's opinion, such quality and standards shall be to his reasonable satisfaction. To the extent that the quality of materials and goods or standards of workmanship are neither described in the Contract Documents nor stated to be a matter for such opinion or satisfaction, they shall be of a standard appropriate to the Works.

     ·2   The Contractor shall take all reasonable steps to encourage Contractor's Persons to be registered cardholders under the Construction Skills Certification Scheme (CSCS) or qualified under an equivalent recognised qualification scheme.

Fees and charges

2·3   The Contractor shall pay all fees and charges in respect of the Works legally recoverable from him. The amount of any such fees or charges (including any rates or taxes other than VAT) shall be added to the Contract Sum unless they are required by the Priced Document or Specification to have been included in the Contract Sum.

Possession

Date of Possession – progress

2·4   On the Date of Possession possession of the site or, in the case of a Section, possession of the relevant part of the site shall be given to the Contractor who shall thereupon begin the construction of the Works or Section and regularly and diligently proceed with and complete the same on or before the relevant Completion Date. For the purposes of the Works insurances the Contractor shall retain possession:

     ·1   of the site and the Works up to and including the date of issue of the Practical Completion Certificate; or

     ·2   of each Section and the relevant part of the site up to and including the date of issue of the Section Completion Certificate for that Section and, in respect of any balance of the site, up to and including the date of issue of the Practical Completion Certificate

and, subject to clause 2·25 and section 8, the Employer shall not be entitled to take possession of any part or parts of the Works or Section until such date.

Deferment of possession

2·5   If the Contract Particulars state that clause 2·5 applies in respect of the Works or any Section, the Employer may defer the giving of possession of the site or relevant part of it for a period not exceeding 6 weeks or lesser period stated in the Contract Particulars, calculated from the relevant Date of Possession.

Early use by Employer

2·6 ·1 Notwithstanding clause 2·4, the Employer may, with the Contractor's consent, use or occupy the site or the Works or part of them, whether for storage or otherwise, before the date of issue of the Practical Completion Certificate or relevant Section Completion Certificate. Before the Contractor gives his consent to such use or occupation, the Contractor or the Employer shall notify the insurers under whichever of Insurance Options A, B or C (paragraph C·2) applies and obtain confirmation that such use or occupation will not prejudice the insurance. Subject to such confirmation, the Contractor's consent shall not be unreasonably delayed or withheld.

·2 Where Insurance Option A applies and the insurers' confirmation is conditional on an additional premium being paid, the Contractor shall notify the Employer of the amount of it. If the Employer continues to require such use or occupation, the additional premium shall be added to the Contract Sum and the Contractor shall if requested produce the receipt for it to the Employer.

Work not forming part of the Contract

2·7 In regard to any work not forming part of this Contract which the Employer requires to be carried out by the Employer himself or by any Employer's Persons:

·1 where the Contract Documents provide the information necessary to enable the Contractor to carry out and complete the Works or each relevant Section in accordance with this Contract, the Contractor shall permit the execution of such work;

·2 where the Contract Documents do not provide the information referred to in clause 2·7·1, the Employer may with the Contractor's consent arrange for the execution of such work, such consent not to be unreasonably delayed or withheld.

Supply of Documents, Setting Out etc.

Contract Documents

2·8 ·1 The Contract Documents and (where Pricing Option B applies) the Priced Document shall remain in the custody of the Employer and shall be available at all reasonable times for inspection by the Contractor.

·2 Immediately after the execution of this Contract the Architect/Contract Administrator, without charge to the Contractor, shall (unless previously provided) provide him with:

·1 one copy, certified on behalf of the Employer, of the Contract Documents; and

·2 two further copies of the Contract Drawings and the Contract Bills/Specification/Work Schedules.

·3 None of the documents referred to in this clause 2·8 or provided or released to the Contractor in accordance with clauses 2·9 to 2·11 shall be used by the Contractor for any purpose other than this Contract, and the Employer, the Architect/Contract Administrator and the Quantity Surveyor shall not divulge or use except for the purposes of this Contract any of the rates or prices in the Priced Document.

Levels and setting out of the Works

2·9 The Architect/Contract Administrator shall determine any levels required for the execution of the Works and shall provide the Contractor by way of accurately dimensioned drawings with such information as shall enable the Contractor to set out the Works. The Contractor shall be responsible for, and shall at no cost to the Employer amend, any errors arising from his own inaccurate setting out. With the Employer's consent, the Architect/Contract Administrator may instruct that such errors shall not be amended and an appropriate deduction shall be made from the Contract Sum for those that are not required to be amended.

Construction information

2·10 Except to the extent that the Architect/Contract Administrator is prevented by an act or default of the Contractor or of any Contractor's Persons, he shall ensure that the information referred to in the Information Release Schedule is released at the time stated in that schedule. The Employer and Contractor may agree to vary any such time, such agreement not to be unreasonably withheld.

Further drawings, details and instructions

2·11 ·1   Where not included in the Information Release Schedule, the Architect/Contract Administrator shall from time to time, without charge to the Contractor, provide him with such further drawings or details as are reasonably necessary to explain and amplify the Contract Drawings and shall issue such instructions (including those for or in regard to the expenditure of Provisional Sums) as are necessary to enable the Contractor to carry out and complete the Works in accordance with this Contract.

       ·2   The further drawings, details and instructions shall be provided or given at the time it is reasonably necessary for the Contractor to receive them, having regard to the progress of the Works, or, if in the Architect/Contract Administrator's opinion practical completion of the Works or relevant Section is likely to be achieved before the relevant Completion Date, having regard to that Completion Date.

       ·3   Where the Contractor has reason to believe that the Architect/Contract Administrator is not aware of the time by which the Contractor needs to receive such further drawings, details or instructions, he shall, so far as reasonably practicable, notify the Architect/Contract Administrator sufficiently in advance as to enable the Architect/Contract Administrator to comply with this clause 2·11.

Errors, Inconsistencies and Divergences

Bills of Quantities

2·12 ·1   Where there are Contract Bills, then, unless in respect of any specified item or items it is otherwise specifically stated in them, those bills are to have been prepared in accordance with the Standard Method of Measurement.

       ·2   If in the Contract Bills there is any unstated departure from the method of preparation referred to in clause 2·12·1 or any error in description or in quantity or any omission of items (including any error in or omission of information in any item which is the subject of a Provisional Sum for defined work), the departure, error or omission shall be corrected. Where the description of a Provisional Sum for defined work does not provide the information required by the Standard Method of Measurement, the description shall be corrected so that it does provide that information.

Instructions on errors, omissions and inconsistencies

2·13 ·1   The Architect/Contract Administrator shall issue instructions in regard to any such departure, error or omission as is referred to in clause 2·12 and in relation to any error in description or quantity, any omission or any inconsistency in or between any of the following documents, namely:

           ·1   the Contract Documents;

           ·2   any instruction issued by the Architect/Contract Administrator under these Conditions; and

           ·3   any drawings or documents issued by the Architect/Contract Administrator under any of clauses 2·9 to 2·11.

       ·2   No such departure, error, omission or inconsistency shall vitiate this Contract.

       ·3   If the Contractor becomes aware of any such departure, error, omission or inconsistency as is referred to in clause 2·12 or 2·13·1 he shall immediately give notice to the Architect/Contract Administrator with appropriate details.

Instructions – additions to Contract Sum, exceptions

2·14   Where instructions under clause 2·13·1 vary the quality or quantity of work included in the Contract Sum, as referred to in clause 4·1, or in any other manner constitute a Variation, they shall be valued in accordance with section 5.

Divergences from Statutory Requirements

2·15 ·1 If the Contractor or Architect/Contract Administrator becomes aware of any divergence between the Statutory Requirements and any of the documents referred to in clause 2·13, he shall immediately give the other notice specifying the divergence.

·2 Within 7 days of becoming aware of such divergence, the Architect/Contract Administrator shall issue instructions in that regard, in relation to which, if and insofar as those instructions require the Works to be varied, they shall be treated as instructions requiring a Variation.

·3 Provided the Contractor is not in breach of clause 2·15·1, the Contractor shall not be liable under this Contract if the Works do not comply with the Statutory Requirements to the extent that the non-compliance results from the Contractor having carried out work in accordance with any of the documents referred to in clauses 2·13·1·1 to 2·13·1·3.

Emergency compliance with Statutory Requirements

2·16 ·1 If in any emergency compliance with the Statutory Requirements necessitates the Contractor supplying materials and/or executing work before receiving instructions under clause 2·15·2, the Contractor shall supply such limited materials and execute such limited work as are reasonably necessary to secure immediate compliance.

·2 The Contractor shall forthwith notify the Architect/Contract Administrator of the emergency and of the steps that he is taking under clause 2·16·1.

·3 Where the emergency has arisen because of a divergence between the Statutory Requirements and any of the documents referred to in clauses 2·13·1·1 to 2·13·1·3, then, provided that the Contractor has complied with clause 2·16·2, work executed and materials supplied by the Contractor under clause 2·16·1 shall be treated as executed and supplied pursuant to an instruction requiring a Variation.

Unfixed Materials and Goods – property, risk etc.

Materials and goods – on site

2·17 Site Materials shall not be removed from storage on or adjacent to the Works except for use on the Works without the Architect/Contract Administrator's consent, such consent not to be unreasonably delayed or withheld. Where their value has in accordance with clause 4·8·1·2 been included in any Interim Certificate under which the amount properly due to the Contractor has been paid by the Employer, they shall upon such payment become the Employer's property, but, subject to Insurance Option B or C (if applicable), the Contractor shall remain responsible for loss or damage to them.

Materials and goods – off site

2·18 Where the value of any Listed Items has in accordance with clause 4·9 been included in any Interim Certificate under which the amount properly due to the Contractor has been paid by the Employer, those items shall become the Employer's property and thereafter the Contractor shall not, except for use upon the Works, remove or cause or permit them to be moved or removed from the premises where they are. The Contractor shall be responsible for any loss of or damage to them and for the cost of their storage, handling and insurance until they are delivered to and placed on or adjacent to the Works. As from such delivery the provisions of clause 2·17 (except the words "Where their value" to "Employer's property, but,") shall apply to such items.

Adjustment of Completion Date

Notice of delay – extensions

2·19 ·1 If and whenever it becomes reasonably apparent that the progress of the Works or any Section is being or is likely to be delayed the Contractor shall forthwith give the Architect/Contract Administrator notice of the cause of the delay. If in the Architect/Contract Administrator's opinion completion of the Works or Section has been, is being or is likely to be delayed beyond the relevant Completion Date by any of the Relevant Events, then, save where these Conditions expressly provide otherwise, the Architect/Contract Administrator, as soon as he is able to estimate the length of the delay beyond that date, shall by notice to the Contractor give a fair and reasonable extension of time for completion of the Works or Section.

continued 2·19

·2   If any Relevant Event referred to in clauses 2·20·1 to 2·20·6 occurs after the relevant Completion Date but before practical completion is achieved, the Architect/Contract Administrator, as soon as he is able to estimate the length of the delay, if any, to the Works or any Section resulting from that event, shall by notice give a fair and reasonable extension of time for completion of the Works or Section.

·3   At any time up to 12 weeks after the date of practical completion of the Works or Section, the Architect/Contract Administrator may give an extension of time in accordance with the provisions of this clause 2·19, whether on reviewing a previous decision or otherwise and whether or not the Contractor has given notice as referred to in clause 2·19·1. Such an extension of time shall not reduce any extension previously given.

·4   Provided always that the Contractor shall:

> ·1   constantly use his best endeavours to prevent delay and do all that may reasonably be required to the satisfaction of the Architect/Contract Administrator to proceed with the Works or Section; and

> ·2   provide such information required by the Architect/Contract Administrator as is reasonably necessary for the purposes of this clause 2·19.

·5   In this clause 2·19 and, so far as relevant, in the other clauses of these Conditions, any reference to delay or extension of time includes any further delay or further extension of time.

Relevant Events

2·20   The following are the Relevant Events referred to in clause 2·19:

·1   Variations and any other matters or instructions which under these Conditions are to be treated as, or as requiring, a Variation;

·2   Architect/Contract Administrator's instructions:

> ·1   under any of clauses 2·13, 3·12 or 3·13 (excluding, where there are Contract Bills, an instruction for expenditure of a Provisional Sum for defined work);

> ·2   (to the extent provided therein) under clause 3·7 and Schedule 2; or

> ·3   for the opening up for inspection or testing of any work, materials or goods under clause 3·14 or 3·15·1 (including making good), unless the inspection or test shows that the work, materials or goods are not in accordance with this Contract;

·3   deferment of the giving of possession of the site or any Section under clause 2·5;

·4   the execution of work for which an Approximate Quantity is not a reasonably accurate forecast of the quantity of work required;

·5   suspension by the Contractor under clause 4·13 of the performance of any or all of his obligations under this Contract;

·6   any impediment, prevention or default, whether by act or omission, by the Employer, the Architect/Contract Administrator, the Quantity Surveyor or any of the Employer's Persons, except to the extent caused or contributed to by any default, whether by act or omission, of the Contractor or of any of the Contractor's Persons;

·7   the carrying out by a Statutory Undertaker of work in pursuance of its statutory obligations in relation to the Works, or the failure to carry out such work;

·8   exceptionally adverse weather conditions;

·9   loss or damage occasioned by any of the Specified Perils;

·10   civil commotion or the use or threat of terrorism and/or the activities of the relevant authorities in dealing with such event or threat;

·11   strike, lock-out or local combination of workmen affecting any of the trades employed upon the Works or any of the trades engaged in the preparation, manufacture or transportation of any of the goods or materials required for the Works;

continued 2·20

·12   the exercise after the Base Date by the United Kingdom Government of any statutory power which directly affects the execution of the Works;

·13   force majeure.

Practical Completion, Lateness and Liquidated Damages

Practical completion and certificates

2·21   When in the Architect/Contract Administrator's opinion practical completion of the Works or a Section is achieved and the Contractor has complied sufficiently with clause 3·18·4, then:

·1   in the case of the Works, the Architect/Contract Administrator shall forthwith issue a certificate to that effect ('the Practical Completion Certificate');

·2   in the case of a Section, he shall forthwith issue a certificate of practical completion of that Section (a 'Section Completion Certificate');

and practical completion of the Works or the Section shall be deemed for all the purposes of this Contract to have taken place on the date stated in that certificate.

Certificate of non-completion

2·22   If the Contractor fails to complete the Works or a Section by the relevant Completion Date, the Architect/Contract Administrator shall issue a certificate to that effect. If an extension of time is made after the issue of such a certificate, the extension shall cancel that certificate and the Architect/Contract Administrator shall where necessary issue a further certificate.

Liquidated damages for non-completion

2·23   ·1   Provided:

·1   the Architect/Contract Administrator has issued a certificate under clause 2·22; and

·2   the Employer has notified the Contractor before the date of the Final Certificate that he may require payment of, or may withhold or deduct, liquidated damages,

the Employer may, not later than 5 days before the final date for payment of the amount payable under clause 4·14, give notice to the Contractor in the terms set out in clause 2·23·2.

·2   A notice from the Employer under clause 2·23·1 shall state that for the period between the Completion Date and the date of practical completion of the Works or that Section:

·1   he requires the Contractor to pay liquidated damages at the rate stated in the Contract Particulars, or lesser rate stated in the notice, in which event the Employer may recover the same as a debt; and/or

·2   that he will withhold or deduct liquidated damages at the rate stated in the Contract Particulars, or at such lesser stated rate, from sums due to the Contractor.[39]

·3   If the Employer in relation to the Works or a Section has notified the Contractor in accordance with clause 2·23·1·2 that he may require payment of, or may withhold or deduct, liquidated damages, then, unless the Employer states otherwise in writing, clause 2·23·1·2 shall remain satisfied in relation to the Works or Section, notwithstanding the cancellation of any certificate and issue of any further certificate under clause 2·22.

Repayment of liquidated damages

2·24   If after the operation of clause 2·23 an extension of time is given and the relevant certificate under clause 2·22 is cancelled the Employer shall pay or repay to the Contractor any amounts deducted or recovered under clause 2·23 in respect of the period of the extension.

---

[39]   In addition to the notice under clause 2·23·2, the Employer, if he intends to withhold or deduct all or any of the liquidated damages payable, must give the appropriate Pay Less Notice under clause 4·11·5, 4·14·4 or 4·14·6·3.

Partial Possession by Employer

Contractor's consent

2·25 If at any time or times before the date of issue by the Architect/Contract Administrator of the Practical Completion Certificate or relevant Section Completion Certificate the Employer wishes to take possession of any part or parts of the Works or a Section and the Contractor's consent has been obtained (which consent shall not be unreasonably delayed or withheld), then, notwithstanding anything expressed or implied elsewhere in this Contract, the Employer may take possession of such part or parts. The Architect/Contract Administrator shall thereupon give the Contractor notice on behalf of the Employer identifying the part or parts taken into possession and giving the date when the Employer took possession ('the Relevant Part' and 'the Relevant Date' respectively).

Practical completion date

2·26 For the purposes of clauses 2·27 and 4·7, practical completion of the Relevant Part shall be deemed to have occurred, and the Rectification Period in respect of the Relevant Part shall be deemed to have commenced, on the Relevant Date.

Defects etc. – Relevant Part

2·27 When in the Architect/Contract Administrator's opinion any defects, shrinkages or other faults in the Relevant Part which he has required to be made good under clause 2·30 have been made good, he shall issue a certificate to that effect.

Insurance – Relevant Part

2·28 As from the Relevant Date the insurance obligation of the Contractor under Insurance Option A or of the Employer under Insurance Option B or paragraph C·2 of Insurance Option C (whichever applies) shall terminate in respect of the Relevant Part (but not otherwise); and where Insurance Option C applies, the obligation of the Employer to insure under paragraph C·1 shall from the Relevant Date include the Relevant Part.

Liquidated damages – Relevant Part

2·29 As from the Relevant Date, the rate of liquidated damages stated in the Contract Particulars in respect of the Works or Section containing the Relevant Part shall reduce by the same proportion as the value of the Relevant Part bears to the Contract Sum or to the relevant Section Sum, as shown in the Contract Particulars.

Defects

Rectification

2·30 Any defects, shrinkages or other faults in the Works or a Section which appear and are notified by the Architect/Contract Administrator to the Contractor not later than 14 days after the expiry of the Rectification Period, and which are due to materials, goods or workmanship not in accordance with this Contract, shall at no cost to the Employer be made good by the Contractor unless the Architect/Contract Administrator with the Employer's consent shall otherwise instruct. If he does so otherwise instruct, an appropriate deduction shall be made from the Contract Sum in respect of the defects, shrinkages or other faults not made good.

Certificate of making good

2·31 The Architect/Contract Administrator shall, when in his opinion the Contractor's obligations under clause 2·30 have been discharged, issue a certificate to that effect.

Access and Representatives

Access for Architect/Contract Administrator

3·1 The Architect/Contract Administrator and any person authorised by him shall at all reasonable times have access to the Works and elsewhere to any work which is being prepared for or is to be utilised in the Works but subject to any reasonable restrictions necessary to protect any proprietary rights.

Person-in-charge

3·2 The Contractor shall ensure that at all reasonable times he has on the site a competent person-in-charge and any instructions given to that person by the Architect/Contract Administrator shall be deemed to have been issued to the Contractor.

Clerk of works

3·3 The Employer shall be entitled to appoint a clerk of works whose duty shall be to act solely as inspector on behalf of the Employer under the Architect/Contract Administrator's directions.

Replacement of Architect/Contract Administrator or Quantity Surveyor

3·4 ·1 If the Architect/Contract Administrator or Quantity Surveyor at any time ceases to hold that post, the Employer shall within 14 days of the cessation nominate a replacement. Except where the Employer is a Local Authority and the nominated replacement is an official of it, if the Contractor objects for reasons considered sufficient by a person appointed under the dispute resolution procedures of this Contract, the Employer shall nominate an acceptable replacement.

·2 No replacement Architect/Contract Administrator appointed for this Contract shall be entitled to disregard or overrule any certificate, opinion, decision or instruction given by any predecessor in that post, save to the extent that that predecessor if still in the post would then have had power under this Contract to do so.

Sub-Contracting

Consent to sub-contracting

3·5 The Contractor shall not without the Architect/Contract Administrator's consent sub-contract the whole or any part of the Works other than in accordance with clause 3·7. Such consent shall not be unreasonably delayed or withheld but any such sub-contracting shall be subject to clause 3·6 and the Contractor shall remain wholly responsible for carrying out and completing the Works in all respects in accordance with clause 2·1 notwithstanding any sub-contracting.

Conditions of sub-contracting

3·6 Where considered appropriate, the Contractor shall engage the Sub-Contractor using the JCT Intermediate Building Sub-Contract. It shall be a condition of any sub-contract that[40]:

·1 the employment of the sub-contractor under the sub-contract shall terminate immediately upon the termination (for any reason) of the Contractor's employment under this Contract;

·2 the sub-contract shall provide:

---

[40] The requirements of clauses 3·6·1 and 3·6·2 together with those in paragraph 3 of the Fluctuations Option (Schedule 4) are met by the JCT Intermediate Sub-Contract ICSub.

continued 3·6·2

·1 that, except for use on the Works, no Site Materials delivered to the Works by or for the sub-contractor shall be removed without the Contractor's written consent (such consent not to be unreasonably delayed or withheld) and that:

·1 where, in accordance with clauses 4·7 and 4·8 of these Conditions, the value of any Site Materials has been included in any Interim Certificate under which the amount properly due to the Contractor has been paid to him, they shall upon such payment become the Employer's property and the sub-contractor shall not deny that they have become the Employer's property;

·2 if the Contractor pays the sub-contractor for any Site Materials before their value is included in any Interim Certificate, they shall upon such payment become the Contractor's property;

·2 for the grant by the sub-contractor of the rights of access to work referred to in clause 3·1 of these Conditions;

·3 that each party undertakes to the other in relation to the Works and the site duly to comply with the CDM Regulations;

·4 that if by the final date for payment stated in the sub-contract the Contractor fails to pay a sum, or any part of it, due to the sub-contractor, the Contractor shall, in addition to any unpaid amount that should properly have been paid, pay simple interest on that amount at the Interest Rate for the period from the final date for payment until such payment is made; such payment of interest to be on and subject to terms equivalent to those of clauses 4·11·6 and 4·14·7 of these Conditions;

·5 where applicable, for the execution and delivery by the sub-contractor, in each case within 14 days of receipt of a written request by the Contractor, of such collateral warranties as comply with the Contract Documents;

·6 that neither of the provisions referred to in clauses 3·6·2·1·1 and 3·6·2·1·2 shall operate so as to affect any vesting in the Contractor of property in any Listed Item required for the purposes of clause 4·9·2·1 of these Conditions.

The Contractor shall not give such consent as is referred to in clause 3·6·2·1 without the prior consent of the Architect/Contract Administrator under clause 2·17 of these Conditions.

Named Sub-Contractors

3·7 Where it is stated in the Contract Bills/Specification/Work Schedules that work described therein for pricing by the Contractor is to be executed by a named person who is to be employed by the Contractor as a sub-contractor (the 'Named Sub-Contractor') the Contractor shall not later than 21 days after entering into this Contract enter into a sub-contract with such person using the Intermediate Named Sub-Contract Agreement ICSub/NAM/A. The provisions of Schedule 2 shall apply with respect to any such sub-contract and with respect to an instruction as to the expenditure of a Provisional Sum under clause 3·13 where the Architect/Contract Administrator requires work to be executed by a named person.

Architect/Contract Administrator's Instructions

Compliance with instructions

3·8 The Contractor shall forthwith comply with all instructions issued to him which the Architect/Contract Administrator is empowered by these Conditions to issue, save that where an instruction requires a Variation of the type referred to in clause 5·1·2, the Contractor need not comply to the extent that he notifies a reasonable objection to it to the Architect/Contract Administrator.

Non-compliance with instructions

3·9 Subject to clause 3·8, if within 7 days after receipt of a notice from the Architect/Contract Administrator requiring compliance with an instruction the Contractor does not comply, the Employer may employ and pay other persons to execute any work whatsoever which may be necessary to give effect to that instruction. The Contractor shall be liable for all additional costs incurred by the Employer in connection with such employment and an appropriate deduction shall be made from the Contract Sum.

Provisions empowering instructions

3·10 On receipt of an instruction or purported instruction the Contractor may request the Architect/Contract Administrator to notify him which provision of these Conditions empowers its issue and the Architect/Contract Administrator shall forthwith comply with the request. If the Contractor thereafter complies with that instruction with neither Party then having invoked any dispute resolution procedure under this Contract to establish the Architect/Contract Administrator's powers in that regard, the instruction shall be deemed to have been duly given under the specified provision.

Instructions requiring Variations

3·11 ·1 The Architect/Contract Administrator may issue instructions requiring a Variation.

·2 Any instruction of the type referred to in clause 5·1·2 shall be subject to the Contractor's right of reasonable objection set out in clause 3·8.

·3 The Architect/Contract Administrator may sanction in writing any Variation made by the Contractor otherwise than pursuant to an instruction.

·4 No Variation required by the Architect/Contract Administrator or subsequently sanctioned by him shall vitiate this Contract.

Postponement of work

3·12 The Architect/Contract Administrator may issue instructions in regard to the postponement of any work to be executed under this Contract.

Instructions on Provisional Sums

3·13 The Architect/Contract Administrator shall issue instructions in regard to the expenditure of Provisional Sums included in the Contract Bills/Specification/Work Schedules.

Inspection – tests

3·14 The Architect/Contract Administrator may issue instructions requiring the Contractor to open up for inspection any work covered up or to arrange for or carry out any test of any materials or goods (whether or not already incorporated in the Works) or of any executed work. The cost of such opening up or testing (including the cost of making good) shall be added to the Contract Sum unless provided for in the Contract Bills/Specification/Work Schedules or unless the inspection or test shows that the materials, goods or work are not in accordance with this Contract.

Work not in accordance with the Contract

3·15 ·1 If during the carrying-out of the Works any work, materials or goods are found not to be in accordance with this Contract, the Contractor shall forthwith notify the Architect/Contract Administrator of the action which the Contractor proposes immediately to take, at no cost to the Employer, to establish that there is no similar failure in work already executed or materials or goods already supplied (whether or not incorporated in the Works). If the Architect/Contract Administrator:

·1 has not received such notification within 7 days of the finding; or

·2 is not satisfied with the action proposed by the Contractor; or

·3 because of safety considerations or statutory obligations, is unable to wait for the Contractor's written proposals,

he may issue instructions requiring the Contractor at no cost to the Employer to open up for inspection any work covered up or to arrange for or carry out any test of any materials or goods (whether or not already incorporated in the Works) or any executed work to establish that there is no similar failure, including making good thereafter. The Contractor shall forthwith comply with any such instruction.

continued 3·15

·2 If within 10 days of receipt of an instruction under clause 3·15·1, and without affecting his obligation to comply with it, the Contractor gives notice to the Architect/Contract Administrator, objecting to compliance and stating his reasons, and if within 7 days of receipt of that objection the Architect/Contract Administrator does not notify withdrawal of the instruction or its modification to remove the Contractor's objection, then any dispute or difference as to whether the nature or the extent of the opening up for inspection or testing instructed by the Architect/Contract Administrator was reasonable in all the circumstances shall be referred to a person appointed under the dispute resolution procedures of this Contract.

·3 If and to the extent that the person appointed finds the instruction was not reasonable he shall decide the amount, if any, to be paid by the Employer to the Contractor in respect of compliance (including making good) and the consequent extension of time, if any, for completion of the Works or any relevant Section.

Instructions as to removal of work etc.

3·16 ·1 The Architect/Contract Administrator may issue instructions in regard to the removal from the site of any work, materials or goods which are not in accordance with this Contract.

·2 If any work is not carried out in a proper and workmanlike manner the Architect/Contract Administrator may issue such instructions to the Contractor as are in consequence reasonably necessary and the Contractor shall comply with them at no cost to the Employer.

Exclusion of persons from the Works

3·17 The Architect/Contract Administrator may (but shall not unreasonably or vexatiously) issue instructions requiring the exclusion from the site of any person employed thereon.

CDM Regulations

Undertakings to comply

3·18 Each Party acknowledges that he is aware of and undertakes to the other that in relation to the Works and site he will duly comply with the CDM Regulations. Without limitation, where the project that comprises or includes the Works is notifiable:

·1 the Employer shall ensure that the CDM Co-ordinator carries out all his duties and, where the Contractor is not the Principal Contractor, shall ensure that the Principal Contractor carries out all his duties under those regulations;

·2 where the Contractor is and while he remains the Principal Contractor, he shall ensure that:

·1 the Construction Phase Plan is prepared and received by the Employer before construction work under this Contract is commenced, and that any subsequent amendment to it by the Contractor is notified to the Employer, the CDM Co-ordinator and (where not the CDM Co-ordinator) the Architect/Contract Administrator; and

·2 welfare facilities complying with Schedule 2 of the CDM Regulations are provided from the commencement of construction work until the end of the construction phase[41];

·3 where the Contractor is not the Principal Contractor, he shall promptly notify the Principal Contractor of the identity of each sub-contractor that he appoints and each sub-subcontractor appointment notified to him;

·4 the Contractor shall promptly upon the written request of the CDM Co-ordinator provide, and shall ensure that any sub-contractor, through the Contractor, provides, to the CDM Co-ordinator (or, if the Contractor is not the Principal Contractor, to the Principal Contractor) such information as the CDM Co-ordinator reasonably requires for the preparation of the health and safety file.

---

[41] There is a duty on contractors to ensure compliance with Schedule 2 of the CDM Regulations so far as is reasonably practicable, whether or not the project is notifiable and whether or not the contractor is the Principal Contractor.

Appointment of successors

3·19   If the Employer by a further appointment replaces the CDM Co-ordinator or the Principal Contractor, the Employer shall immediately upon such further appointment notify the Contractor of the name and address of the new appointee. If the Employer appoints a successor to the Contractor as the Principal Contractor, the Contractor shall at no cost to the Employer comply with all reasonable requirements of the new Principal Contractor to the extent necessary for compliance with the CDM Regulations; no extension of time shall be given in respect of such compliance.

Contract Sum and Adjustment

Work included in Contract Sum

4·1   ·1   Where there are Contract Bills, the quality and quantity of the work included in the Contract Sum shall be that set out in those bills.

         ·2   Where there are no Contract Bills and save insofar as quantities are given in the Specification or Work Schedules, the quality and quantity of the work included in the Contract Sum shall be that set out in the Contract Documents taken together, provided that if work stated or shown on the Contract Drawings is inconsistent with the description (if any) of that work in the Specification or Work Schedules, then that stated or shown on the Contract Drawings shall prevail.

         ·3   Where there are no Contract Bills, but quantities are given for any items in the Specification or Work Schedules, the quality and quantity of the work included in the Contract Sum for those items shall be that set out in the Specification or Work Schedules.

Adjustment only under the Conditions

4·2   The Contract Sum shall not be adjusted or altered in any way other than in accordance with clause 4·3 and other express provisions of these Conditions and, subject to clause 2·13, any error in the computation of the Contract Sum is accepted by the Parties.

Adjustment of Contract Sum

4·3   ·1   The Contract Sum shall be adjusted by:

            ·1   each amount agreed by the Employer and the Contractor in respect of Variations and other work of the types referred to in clause 5·2 or the amount of any Valuation;

            ·2   the amounts referred to in clause 4·8·2 and the deductions referred to in clause 4·8·3, each as finally ascertained;

            ·3   the deduction of all Provisional Sums and the value of any work for which an Approximate Quantity is included in the Contract Documents;

            ·4   the amount of any deduction under clause 2·30; and

            ·5   any amounts to be included as a result of costs incurred by the Contractor under clause 6·15.

         ·2   Not later than 6 months after the issue of the Practical Completion Certificate or the Section Completion Certificate, the Contractor shall provide the Architect/Contract Administrator, or (if so instructed) the Quantity Surveyor, with all documents reasonably required for the adjustment of the Contract Sum. Not later than 3 months after receipt of those documents a statement of all the final Valuations under section 5 shall be prepared by the Quantity Surveyor and copies of that statement and the computations of the adjusted Contract Sum shall within that 3 month period be sent to the Contractor.

Payments, Certificates and Notices

VAT

4·4   ·1   The Contract Sum is exclusive of VAT and in relation to any payment to the Contractor under this Contract, the Employer shall in addition pay the amount of any VAT properly chargeable in respect of it.

continued 4·4

·2   To the extent that after the Base Date the supply of goods and services to the Employer becomes exempt from VAT there shall be paid to the Contractor an amount equal to the amount of input tax on the supply to the Contractor of goods and services which contribute to the Works but which as a consequence of that exemption the Contractor cannot recover.

Construction Industry Scheme (CIS)

4·5   If the Employer is or at any time up to the payment of the Final Certificate becomes a 'contractor' for the purposes of the CIS[42], his obligation to make any payment under this Contract is subject to the provisions of the CIS.

Advance payment

4·6   Where the Contract Particulars state that clause 4·6 applies, the advance payment shall be paid to the Contractor on the date and reimbursed to the Employer on the terms stated in the Contract Particulars. Provided that where the Contract Particulars state that an advance payment bond is required, payment shall only be made if the Contractor has provided to the Employer a bond in the terms set out in Part 1 of Schedule 3 from a surety approved by the Employer.

Interim payments – due dates and certificates

4·7   ·1   Subject to any agreement between the Parties as to stage payments, the due dates for interim payments by the Employer are:

·1   for the period up to the date of practical completion of the Works, the monthly dates specified in the Contract Particulars;

·2   a date not later than 14 days after the date of practical completion;

·3   thereafter, the specified dates at intervals of 2 months; and

·4   the date of expiry of the Rectification Period or, if later, the date of issue of the certificate of making good (or, where there are Sections, the last such period or certificate).

·2   The Architect/Contract Administrator shall not later than 5 days after each due date issue an Interim Certificate, stating the sum that he considers to be or have been due at the due date to the Contractor in respect of the interim payment, calculated in accordance with clause 4·8, and the basis on which that sum has been calculated.

·3   Interim valuations shall be made by the Quantity Surveyor whenever the Architect/Contract Administrator considers them necessary for ascertaining the amount to be stated as due in an interim payment.

Interim payments – amounts due

4·8   The amount of each interim payment to be certified under clause 4·7·2 shall be the total of the amounts referred to in clauses 4·8·1 and 4·8·2 less the total of the amounts referred to in clause 4·8·3, at a date not more than 7 days before the due date of an interim payment, less the cumulative total of the amounts of any advance payment that have then become due for reimbursement to the Employer in accordance with the terms stated in the Contract Particulars for clause 4·6 and less the total of sums stated as due in previous Interim Certificates and any sums paid in respect of an Interim Payment Notice given after the issue of the latest Interim Certificate. The amounts referred to are:

·1   the applicable percentage, as stated in the Contract Particulars, of the total value of:

·1   the work properly executed by the Contractor, including any work so executed for which a value has been agreed pursuant to clause 5·2·1 or which has been valued under the Valuation Rules, but excluding any restoration or other work under Schedule 1, as referred to in clause 4·8·2. Where there is an Activity Schedule, the value to be included in respect of the work in each activity to which it relates shall be a proportion of the price stated for the work in that activity equal to the proportion of the work in that activity that has then been properly executed;

---

[42]   See the Contract Particulars (Fifth Recital and clause 4·5).

continued 4·8·1

·2 Site Materials, provided that their value shall only be included if they are adequately protected against weather and other casualties and they are not on the Works prematurely; and

·3 any Listed Items, when their value is to be included under clause 4·9;

·2 the full amount (100%) (to the extent then ascertained) payable to the Contractor or to be added to the Contract Sum in respect of:

Fees and charges (clause 2·3);
Inspection and testing (clauses 3·14 and 3·15·3);
Costs and expenses (clause 4·13);
Fluctuations – Contribution, levy and tax fluctuations, if applicable (clause 4·15);
Fluctuations – Named Sub-Contractors (clause 4·16);
Loss and Expense (clause 4·17);
Insurance premiums (clauses 2·6, 6·5, 6·10 and 6·11 and paragraph B·2·1 or C·3·1 of Schedule 1);
Restoration etc. of loss or damage (paragraph A·4·4, B·3·5 or C·4·5 of Schedule 1);

·3 the ascertained amount of any deductions to be made under clause 2·9 *(Levels)*, 2·30 *(Rectification)*, 3·9 *(Non-compliance with instructions)*, 4·15 or 4·16 *(Fluctuations)* or (in the event of a reduction in the premium) 6·10 *(Terrorism Cover premiums)*.

Off-site materials and goods

4·9 The sum stated as due in an Interim Certificate shall include the value of any Listed Items before their delivery to or adjacent to the Works provided that the following conditions have been fulfilled:

·1 the Listed Items are in accordance with this Contract;

·2 the Contractor has provided the Architect/Contract Administrator with reasonable proof that:

·1 the property in the Listed Items is vested in the Contractor; and

·2 the Listed Items are insured against loss or damage for their full value under a policy of insurance protecting the interests of the Employer and the Contractor in respect of the Specified Perils, during the period commencing with the transfer of property in the Listed Items to the Contractor until they are delivered to, or adjacent to, the Works;

·3 at the premises where the Listed Items have been manufactured or assembled or are stored, there is in relation to those items clear identification of:

·1 the Employer as the person to whose order they are held; and

·2 their destination as the Works,

and the items either are set apart or have been clearly and visibly marked, individually or in sets, by letters or figures or by reference to a pre-determined code; and

·4 in the case of uniquely identified Listed Items, the Contractor, if it is stated in the Contract Particulars as required, has provided a bond in favour of the Employer from a surety approved by the Employer in the terms set out in Part 2 of Schedule 3 ('the required bond') in the amount specified in the Contract Particulars for this clause 4·9·4; or

·5 in the case of Listed Items which are not uniquely identified, the Contractor has provided the required bond in the amount specified in the Contract Particulars for this clause 4·9·5.

Contractor's Interim Applications and Payment Notices

4·10 ·1 In relation to any interim payment the Contractor may not less than 7 days before the due date make an application to the Quantity Surveyor (an 'Interim Application'), stating the sum that the Contractor considers will become due to him at the relevant due date in accordance with clause 4·8 and the basis on which that sum has been calculated.

·2 If an Interim Certificate is not issued in accordance with clause 4·7·2, then:

·1 where the Contractor has made an Interim Application in accordance with clause 4·10·1, that application is for the purposes of these Conditions an Interim Payment Notice; or

continued 4·10·2

·2   where the Contractor has not made an Interim Application, he may at any time after the 5 day period referred to in clause 4·7·2 give an Interim Payment Notice to the Quantity Surveyor, stating the sum that the Contractor considers to be or have been due to him at the relevant due date in accordance with clause 4·8 and the basis on which that sum has been calculated.

Interim payments – final date and amount

4·11   ·1   Subject to clause 4·11·4, the final date for payment of an interim payment shall be 14 days from its due date.

·2   Subject to any Pay Less Notice given by the Employer under clause 4·11·5, the sum to be paid by the Employer on or before the final date for payment shall be the sum stated as due in the Interim Certificate.

·3   If the Interim Certificate is not issued in accordance with clause 4·7·2, but an Interim Payment Notice has been given under clause 4·10, the sum to be paid by the Employer shall, subject to any Pay Less Notice under clause 4·11·5, be the sum stated as due in the Interim Payment Notice.

·4   Where an Interim Payment Notice is given under clause 4·10·2·2, the final date for payment of the sum specified in it shall for all purposes be regarded as postponed by the same number of days as the number of days after expiry of the 5 day period referred to in clause 4·7·2 that the Interim Payment Notice is given.

·5   If the Employer intends to pay less than the sum stated as due from him in the Interim Certificate or Interim Payment Notice, as the case may be, he shall not later than 5 days before the final date for payment give the Contractor notice of that intention in accordance with clause 4·12·1 (a 'Pay Less Notice'). Where a Pay Less Notice is given, the payment to be made on or before the final date for payment shall not be less than the amount stated as due in the notice.

·6   If the Employer fails to pay a sum, or any part of it, due to the Contractor under these Conditions by the final date for its payment, the Employer shall, in addition to any unpaid amount that should properly have been paid, pay the Contractor simple interest on that amount at the Interest Rate for the period from the final date for payment until payment is made. Interest under this clause 4·11·6 shall be a debt due to the Contractor from the Employer.

·7   Acceptance of a payment of interest under clause 4·11·6 shall not in any circumstances be construed as a waiver of the Contractor's right to proper payment of the principal amount due, to suspend performance under clause 4·13 or to terminate his employment under section 8.

Pay Less Notices and general provisions

4·12   ·1   A Pay Less Notice:

     ·1   (where it is to be given by the Employer) shall specify both the sum that he considers to be due to the Contractor at the date the notice is given and the basis on which that sum has been calculated, and may be given on behalf of the Employer by the Architect/Contract Administrator or Quantity Surveyor or by any other person who the Employer notifies the Contractor as being authorised to do so;

     ·2   (where it is to be given by the Contractor) shall be sent to the Employer, with a copy to the Architect/Contract Administrator, and shall specify both the sum that the Contractor considers to be due to the Employer at that date and the basis on which that sum has been calculated;

     ·3   may not be given in relation to a payment for which an Interim Certificate or the Final Certificate has not been issued until the Contractor has in respect of the payment given an Interim Payment Notice or Final Payment Notice.

·2   In relation to the requirements for the issue of certificates and the giving of notices under section 4, it is immaterial that the amount then considered to be due may be zero.

continued 4·12

·3 Where the Employer is not a Local Authority, the Employer's interest in the percentage of the total value not included in the amounts of the interim payments to be certified under clause 4·7·2 shall be fiduciary as trustee for the Contractor (but without obligation to invest) and the Contractor's beneficial interest in that sum shall be subject only to the right of the Employer to have recourse to it from time to time for payment of any amount which he is entitled under the provisions of this Contract to withhold or deduct from sums due or to become due to the Contractor.

Contractor's right of suspension

4·13 ·1 Without affecting the Contractor's other rights and remedies, if the Employer fails to pay the Contractor the sum payable in accordance with clause 4·11 (together with any VAT properly chargeable in respect of such payment) by the final date for payment and the failure continues for 7 days after the Contractor has given notice to the Employer, with a copy to the Architect/Contract Administrator, of his intention to suspend the performance of his obligations under this Contract and the ground or grounds on which it is intended to suspend performance, the Contractor may suspend performance of any or all of those obligations until payment is made in full.

·2 Where the Contractor exercises his right of suspension under clause 4·13·1, he shall be entitled to a reasonable amount in respect of costs and expenses reasonably incurred by him as a result of the exercise of the right.

·3 Applications in respect of any such costs and expenses shall be made to the Architect/Contract Administrator and the Contractor shall with his application or on request submit such details of the costs and expenses as are reasonably necessary to enable his entitlement to be ascertained.

Final Certificate and final payment[43]

4·14 ·1 The Architect/Contract Administrator shall issue the Final Certificate not later than 28 days after whichever of the following occurs last:

·1 the end of the Rectification Period in respect of the Works or (where there are Sections) the last such period to expire;

·2 the date of issue of the certificate of making good under clause 2·31 or (where there are Sections) the last such certificate to be issued; or

·3 the date on which the Architect/Contract Administrator sends to the Contractor copies of the statement and computations of the adjusted Contract Sum under clause 4·3·2.

·2 The Final Certificate shall state:

·1 the Contract Sum as adjusted in accordance with clause 4·3·1; and

·2 the sum of amounts already stated as due in Interim Certificates plus the amount of any advance payment paid pursuant to clause 4·6 and (where relevant) any sums paid in respect of any such Interim Payment Notice as is referred to in clause 4·8,

and (without affecting the rights of the Contractor in respect of any interim payment not paid in full by the Employer by its final date for payment) the final payment shall be the difference (if any) between the two sums, which shall be shown in the Final Certificate as a balance due to the Contractor from the Employer or to the Employer from the Contractor, as the case may be. The Final Certificate shall state the basis on which that amount has been calculated.

·3 The due date for the final payment shall be the date of issue of the Final Certificate or, if that certificate is not issued within the 28 day period referred to in clause 4·14·1, the last day of that period and, subject to clause 4·14·6, the final date for payment shall be 28 days from its due date.

·4 If the Party by whom the final payment is stated to be payable ('the payer') intends to pay less than the stated balance, he shall not later than 5 days before the final date for payment give the other Party a Pay Less Notice in accordance with clause 4·12·1.

---

[43] The effect of the Final Certificate is set out in clause 1·9.

·5   Where a Pay Less Notice is given under clause 4·14·4, the payment to be made on or before the final date for payment shall not be less than the amount stated as due in the notice.

·6   If the Final Certificate is not issued in accordance with clauses 4·14·1 and 4·14·2:

    ·1   the Contractor may at any time after expiry of the 28 day period referred to in clause 4·14·1 give notice to the Employer with a copy to the Architect/Contract Administrator (a 'Final Payment Notice') stating what the Contractor considers to be the amount of the final payment due to him under this Contract and the basis on which the sum has been calculated and, subject to any Pay Less Notice given under clause 4·14·6·3, the final payment shall be that amount;

    ·2   if the Contractor gives a Final Payment Notice, the final date for payment of the sum specified in it shall for all purposes be regarded as postponed by the same number of days as the number of days after expiry of the 28 day period that the Final Payment Notice is given;

    ·3   following the Final Payment Notice the Employer may not later than 5 days before the final date for payment give a Pay Less Notice in accordance with clause 4·12·1 and, if he gives such notice, the provisions of clause 4·14·5 shall correspondingly apply.

·7   If the payer fails to pay the final payment, or any part of it, by the final date for its payment, he shall, in addition to any unpaid amount that should properly have been paid, pay the other Party simple interest on that amount at the Interest Rate for the period from the final date for payment until payment is made.

·8   Acceptance of a payment of interest under this clause 4·14 shall not in any circumstances be construed as a waiver of any right to proper payment of the principal amount due.

·9   The final payment and any interest under this clause 4·14 shall be a debt due from the payer to the other Party.

Fluctuations

Contribution, levy and tax fluctuations

4·15   Contribution, levy and tax changes shall be dealt with by the application of Schedule 4 (*Fluctuations Option*), unless the Contract Particulars entry is deleted.

Fluctuations – Named Sub-Contractors

4·16   In respect of any amount included in the Contract Sum for work to be executed by a Named Sub-Contractor, the Contract Sum shall be adjusted by the net amount payable to or allowable by him under the applicable Fluctuations Option of the Named Sub-Contract Conditions excluding any amount that arises from any extension of the period or periods for completion of the Sub-Contract Works due to an impediment, prevention or default, whether by act or omission, by the Contractor or any of the Contractor's Persons.

Loss and Expense

Disturbance of regular progress

4·17   If in the execution of this Contract the Contractor incurs or is likely to incur direct loss and/or expense for which he would not be reimbursed by a payment under any other provision in these Conditions due to:

    ·1   a deferment of giving possession of the site or relevant part of it under clause 2·5; or

    ·2   the regular progress of the Works or any part of them being materially affected by any of the Relevant Matters,

continued 4·17

and the Contractor makes an application to the Architect/Contract Administrator within a reasonable time of that becoming apparent, then, save where these Conditions provide that there shall be no addition to the Contract Sum or otherwise exclude the operation of this clause, the Architect/Contract Administrator, if and as soon as he is of that opinion, shall ascertain, or instruct the Quantity Surveyor to ascertain, the amount of the loss and/or expense incurred and that amount shall be added to the Contract Sum, provided that the Contractor shall in support of his application submit such information required by the Architect/Contract Administrator or the Quantity Surveyor as is reasonably necessary for the purposes of this clause 4·17.

Relevant Matters

4·18   The following are the Relevant Matters:

·1   Variations (including any other matters or instructions which under these Conditions are to be treated as, or as requiring, a Variation);

·2   Architect/Contract Administrator's instructions:

·1   under clause 3·12 or 3·13 (excluding, where there are Contract Bills, an instruction for expenditure of a Provisional Sum for defined work);

·2   (to the extent provided therein) under clause 3·7 and Schedule 2;

·3   for the opening up for inspection or testing of any work, materials or goods under clause 3·14 (including making good), unless the inspection or test shows that the work, materials or goods are not in accordance with this Contract; or

·4   in relation to errors, omissions and inconsistencies in or between the Contract Documents and/or other documents referred to in clause 2·13;

·3   the execution of work for which an Approximate Quantity is not a reasonably accurate forecast of the quantity of work required;

·4   any impediment, prevention or default, whether by act or omission, by the Employer, the Architect/Contract Administrator, the Quantity Surveyor or any of the Employer's Persons, except to the extent caused or contributed to by any default, whether by act or omission, of the Contractor or of any of the Contractor's Persons.

Reservation of Contractor's rights and remedies

4·19   The provisions of clauses 4·17 and 4·18 are without prejudice to any other rights and remedies which the Contractor may possess.

General

Definition of Variations

5·1   The term 'Variation' means:

·1   the alteration or modification of the design, quality or quantity of the Works including:

·1   the addition, omission or substitution of any work;

·2   the alteration of the kind or standard of any of the materials or goods to be used in the Works;

·3   the removal from the site of any work executed or Site Materials other than work, materials or goods which are not in accordance with this Contract;

·2   the imposition by the Employer of any obligations or restrictions in regard to the matters set out in this clause 5·1·2 or the addition to or alteration or omission of any such obligations or restrictions so imposed or imposed by the Employer in the Contract Documents in regard to:

·1   access to the site or use of any specific parts of the site;

·2   limitations of working space;

·3   limitations of working hours; or

·4   the execution or completion of the work in any specific order.[44]

Valuation of Variations and provisional sum work

5·2   The value of:

·1   all Variations required by Architect/Contract Administrator's instructions or subsequently sanctioned by him in writing;

·2   all work which under these Conditions is to be treated as a Variation;

·3   all work executed by the Contractor in accordance with Architect/Contract Administrator's instructions as to the expenditure of Provisional Sums included in the Priced Document; and

·4   all work executed by the Contractor for which an Approximate Quantity has been included in the Priced Document

shall be such amount as is agreed by the Employer and the Contractor or, where not agreed, shall, unless otherwise agreed by the Employer and the Contractor, be the amount valued by the Quantity Surveyor (a 'Valuation') in accordance with clauses 5·3 to 5·6 ('the Valuation Rules').

The Valuation Rules

Measurable Work

5·3   ·1   To the extent that a Valuation relates to the execution of additional or substituted work which can properly be valued by measurement or to the execution of work for which an Approximate Quantity is included in Contract Bills, such work shall be measured and shall be valued in accordance with the following rules:

---

[44]   See clause 3·8·1 for the Contractor's right of reasonable objection to Variations within clause 5·1·2.

continued 5·3·1

·1   where the additional or substituted work is of similar character to, is executed under similar conditions as, and does not significantly change the quantity of, work set out in the Contract Documents, the rates and prices for the work set out in the Priced Document shall determine the valuation;

·2   where the additional or substituted work is of similar character to work set out in the Contract Documents but is not executed under similar conditions thereto and/or significantly changes its quantity, the rates and prices for the work set out in the Priced Document shall be the basis for determining the valuation and the Valuation shall include a fair allowance for such difference in conditions and/or quantity;

·3   where the additional or substituted work is not of similar character to work set out in the Priced Document, the work shall be valued at fair rates and prices;

·4   where the Approximate Quantity is a reasonably accurate forecast of the quantity of work required the rate or price for the Approximate Quantity shall determine the valuation; and

·5   where the Approximate Quantity is not a reasonably accurate forecast of the quantity of work required, the rate or price for that Approximate Quantity shall be the basis for determining the valuation and the Valuation shall include a fair allowance for such difference in quantity.

Provided that clauses 5·3·1·4 and 5·3·1·5 shall apply only to the extent that the work has not been altered or modified other than in quantity.

·2   To the extent that a Valuation relates to the omission of work set out in the Contract Documents, the rates and prices for such work therein set out shall determine the valuation of the work omitted.

·3   In any valuation of work under clauses 5·3·1 and 5·3·2:

·1   measurement shall be in accordance with the same principles as those governing the preparation of Contract Bills, as referred to in clause 2·12;

·2   allowance shall be made for any percentage or lump sum adjustments in the Priced Document; and

·3   allowance, where appropriate, shall be made for any addition to or reduction of preliminary items of the type referred to in the Standard Method of Measurement, provided that no such allowance shall be made in respect of compliance with an Architect/Contract Administrator's instruction for the expenditure of a Provisional Sum for defined work.

Daywork

5·4   Where the execution of additional or substituted work cannot be valued in accordance with clause 5·3, the Valuation shall comprise:

·1   the prime cost of such work (calculated in accordance with the 'Definition of Prime Cost of Daywork carried out under a Building Contract' issued by The Royal Institution of Chartered Surveyors (RICS) and the Construction Confederation as current at the Base Date) together with Percentage Additions to each section of the prime cost at the rates stated in the Priced Document or, if they apply in respect of labour, at the All-Inclusive Rates stated therein; or

·2   where the work is within the province of any specialist trade and the RICS and the appropriate body representing the employers in that trade have agreed and issued a definition of prime cost of daywork[45], the prime cost of such work calculated in accordance with that definition current at the Base Date, together with Percentage Additions on the prime cost at the rates stated in the Priced Document or, if they apply in respect of labour, at the All-Inclusive Rates stated therein.

---

[45]   There are currently three definitions to which clause 5·4·2 refers, namely those agreed between the RICS and the Electrical Contractors Association, the RICS and the Electrical Contractors Association of Scotland and the RICS and the Heating and Ventilating Contractors Association.

continued 5·4

Provided that in any case vouchers specifying the time daily spent upon the work, the workmen's names, the plant and the materials employed shall be delivered for verification to the Architect/Contract Administrator or his authorised representative not later than 7 Business Days after the work has been executed.

Change of conditions for other work

5·5   If as a result of:

·1   compliance with any instruction requiring a Variation;

·2   compliance with any instruction as to the expenditure of a Provisional Sum for undefined work;

·3   compliance with any instruction as to the expenditure of a Provisional Sum for defined work, to the extent that the instruction for that work differs from the description given for such work in Contract Bills; or

·4   the execution of work for which an Approximate Quantity is included in Contract Bills, to the extent that the quantity is more or less than the quantity ascribed to that work in Contract Bills,

there is a substantial change in the conditions under which any other work is executed, then such other work shall be treated as if it had been the subject of an instruction requiring a Variation and shall be valued in accordance with the provisions of this section 5.

Additional provisions

5·6   ·1   To the extent that a Valuation does not relate to the execution of additional or substituted work or the omission of work or to the extent that the valuation of any work or liabilities directly associated with a Variation cannot reasonably be effected in the Valuation by the application of clauses 5·3 to 5·5, a fair valuation shall be made.

·2   No allowance shall be made under the Valuation Rules for any effect upon the regular progress of the Works or of any part of them or for any other direct loss and/or expense for which the Contractor would be reimbursed by payment under any other provision in these Conditions.

Injury to Persons and Property

Liability of Contractor – personal injury or death

6·1   The Contractor shall be liable for, and shall indemnify the Employer against, any expense, liability, loss, claim or proceedings whatsoever in respect of personal injury to or the death of any person arising out of or in the course of or caused by the carrying out of the Works, except to the extent that the same is due to any act or neglect of the Employer, of any of the Employer's Persons or of any Statutory Undertaker.

Liability of Contractor – injury or damage to property

6·2   The Contractor shall be liable for, and shall indemnify the Employer against, any expense, liability, loss, claim or proceedings in respect of any loss, injury or damage whatsoever to any property real or personal in so far as such loss, injury or damage arises out of or in the course of or by reason of the carrying out of the Works and to the extent that the same is due to any negligence, breach of statutory duty, omission or default of the Contractor or of any of the Contractor's Persons. This liability and indemnity is subject to clause 6·3 and, where Insurance Option C (Schedule 1, paragraph C·1) applies, excludes loss or damage to any property required to be insured thereunder caused by a Specified Peril.

Injury or damage to property – Works and Site Materials excluded

6·3   ·1   Subject to clauses 6·3·2 and 6·3·3, the reference in clause 6·2 to 'property real or personal' does not include the Works, work executed and/or Site Materials up to and including whichever is the earlier of:

       ·1   the date of issue of the Practical Completion Certificate; or

       ·2   the date of termination of the Contractor's employment.

   ·2   Where a Section Completion Certificate is issued in respect of a Section, that Section shall not after the date of issue of that certificate be regarded as 'the Works' or 'work executed' for the purpose of clause 6·3·1.

   ·3   If clause 2·25 has been operated, then, after the Relevant Date, the Relevant Part shall not be regarded as 'the Works' or 'work executed' for the purpose of clause 6·3·1.

Insurance against Personal Injury and Property Damage

Contractor's insurance of his liability

6·4   ·1   Without prejudice to his obligation to indemnify the Employer under clauses 6·1 and 6·2, the Contractor shall take out and maintain insurance in respect of claims arising out of his liability referred to in clauses 6·1 and 6·2 which:

       ·1   in respect of claims for personal injury to or the death of any employee of the Contractor arising out of and in the course of such person's employment, shall comply with all relevant legislation; and

continued 6·4·1

·2   for all other claims to which clause 6·4·1 applies[46], shall indemnify the Employer in like manner to the Contractor (but only to the extent that the Contractor may be liable to indemnify the Employer under the terms of this Contract) and shall be in a sum not less than that stated in the Contract Particulars for any one occurrence or series of occurrences arising out of one event.[47]

·2   As and when reasonably required to do so by the Employer, the Contractor shall send to the Architect/Contract Administrator for inspection by the Employer documentary evidence that the insurances required by clause 6·4·1 have been taken out and are being maintained, and at any time the Employer may (but shall not unreasonably or vexatiously) require that the relevant policy or policies and related premium receipts be sent to the Architect/Contract Administrator for such inspection.

·3   If the Contractor defaults in taking out or in maintaining insurance in accordance with clause 6·4·1 the Employer may himself insure against any liability or expense which he may incur as a result of such default and the amount paid or payable by him in respect of premiums therefor may be deducted from any sums due or to become due to the Contractor under this Contract or shall be recoverable from the Contractor as a debt.

Contractor's insurance of liability of Employer

6·5   ·1   If the Contract Particulars state that insurance under clause 6·5·1 may be required, the Contractor shall, if instructed by the Architect/Contract Administrator, take out a policy of insurance in the names of the Employer and the Contractor[48] for the amount of indemnity there stated in respect of any expense, liability, loss, claim or proceedings which the Employer may incur or sustain by reason of injury or damage to any property caused by collapse, subsidence, heave, vibration, weakening or removal of support or lowering of ground water arising out of or in the course of or by reason of the carrying out of the Works, excluding injury or damage:

·1   for which the Contractor is liable under clause 6·2; or

·2   which is attributable to errors or omissions in the designing of the Works; or

·3   which can reasonably be foreseen to be inevitable having regard to the nature of the work to be executed and the manner of its execution; or

·4   (if Insurance Option C applies) which it is the responsibility of the Employer to insure under paragraph C·1 of Schedule 1; or

·5   to the Works and Site Materials except where the Practical Completion Certificate has been issued or in so far as any Section is the subject of a Section Completion Certificate; or

·6   which arises from any consequence of war, invasion, act of foreign enemy, hostilities (whether war is declared or not), civil war, rebellion or revolution, insurrection or military or usurped power; or

·7   which is directly or indirectly caused by or contributed to by or arises from the Excepted Risks; or

---

[46]   It should be noted that the cover granted under public liability policies taken out pursuant to clause 6·4·1 may not be co-extensive with the indemnity given to the Employer in clauses 6·1 and 6·2: for example, each claim may be subject to the excess in the policy and cover may not be available in respect of loss or damage due to gradual pollution.

[47]   The Contractor may, if he wishes, insure for a sum greater than that stated in the Contract Particulars.

[48]   A policy of insurance taken out for the purposes of clause 6·5 should not have an expiry date earlier than the end of the Rectification Period.

continued 6·5·1

·8   which is directly or indirectly caused by or arises out of pollution or contamination of buildings or other structures or of water or land or the atmosphere happening during the period of insurance, save that this exception shall not apply in respect of pollution or contamination caused by a sudden identifiable, unintended and unexpected incident which takes place in its entirety at a specific moment in time and place during the period of insurance (all pollution or contamination which arises out of one incident being considered for the purpose of this insurance to have occurred at the time such incident takes place); or

·9   which results in any costs or expenses being incurred by the Employer or in any other sums being payable by the Employer in respect of damages for breach of contract, except to the extent that such costs or expenses or damages would have attached in the absence of any contract.

·2   Any insurance under clause 6·5·1 shall be placed with insurers approved by the Employer, and the Contractor shall send to the Architect/Contract Administrator for deposit with the Employer the policy or policies and related premium receipts.

·3   The amounts expended by the Contractor to take out and maintain the insurance referred to in clause 6·5·1 shall be added to the Contract Sum.

Excepted Risks

6·6   Notwithstanding clauses 6·1, 6·2 and 6·4·1, the Contractor shall not be liable either to indemnify the Employer or to insure against any personal injury to or the death of any person or any damage, loss or injury to the Works, Site Materials, work executed, the site or any other property, caused by the effect of an Excepted Risk.

Insurance of the Works

Insurance Options

6·7   Insurance Options A, B and C are set out in Schedule 1. The Insurance Option that applies to this Contract is that stated in the Contract Particulars.[49]

Related definitions

6·8   In Schedule 1 and, so far as relevant, in the clauses of these Conditions the following phrases shall have the meanings given below:

All Risks Insurance[50]:   insurance which provides cover against any physical loss or damage to work executed and Site Materials and against the reasonable cost of the removal and disposal of debris and of any shoring and propping of the Works which results from such physical loss or damage but excluding the cost necessary to repair, replace or rectify:

(a)   property which is defective due to:

(i)   wear and tear,

---

[49]   **Insurance Option A** is applicable to the erection of new buildings where the **Contractor** is required to take out a Joint Names Policy for All Risks Insurance of the Works and **Insurance Option B** is applicable where the **Employer** has elected to take out that Joint Names Policy. **Insurance Option C** is for use in the case of alterations of or extensions to existing structures; under it, the **Employer** is required to take out a Joint Names Policy for All Risks Insurance for the Works and also a Joint Names Policy to insure the existing structures and their contents owned by him or for which he is responsible against loss or damage by the Specified Perils. Some Employers (e.g. tenants and homeowners) may not be able readily to obtain the Joint Names cover, in particular that under paragraph C·1. If so, Option C should not be stated to apply and consequential amendments may be necessary. See the Intermediate Building Contract Guide.

[50]   The risks and costs that All Risks Insurance is required to cover are defined by exclusions. Policies issued by insurers are not standardised; the way in which insurance for these risks is expressed varies and **in some cases it may not be possible for insurance to be taken out against certain of the risks required to be covered.** In the case of Terrorism Cover, where the extension of cover will involve an additional premium and may in certain situations be difficult to effect, the requirement is now expressly limited to Pool Re Cover or such other cover as is agreed and set out in the Contract Particulars. That extension and any other relevant details of Works insurance require discussion and agreement between the Parties and their insurance advisers **prior to entering into the Contract.** See the Intermediate Building Contract Guide.

continued 6·8

      (ii)   obsolescence, or

      (iii)   deterioration, rust or mildew;

(b) any work executed or any Site Materials lost or damaged as a result of its own defect in design, plan, specification, material or workmanship or any other work executed which is lost or damaged in consequence thereof where such work relied for its support or stability on such work which was defective[51];

(c) loss or damage caused by or arising from:

      (i)   any consequence of war, invasion, act of foreign enemy, hostilities (whether war be declared or not), civil war, rebellion, revolution, insurrection, military or usurped power, confiscation, commandeering, nationalisation or requisition or loss or destruction of or damage to any property by or under the order of any government *de jure* or *de facto* or public, municipal or local authority,

      (ii)   disappearance or shortage if such disappearance or shortage is only revealed when an inventory is made or is not traceable to an identifiable event, or

      (iii) an Excepted Risk.

Excepted Risks: the risks comprise:

(a) ionising radiations or contamination by radioactivity from any nuclear fuel or from any nuclear waste from the combustion of nuclear fuel, radioactive toxic explosive or other hazardous properties of any explosive nuclear assembly or nuclear component thereof (other than such risk insofar, but only insofar, as it is included in the Terrorism Cover from time to time required to be taken out and maintained under this Contract);

(b) pressure waves caused by aircraft or other aerial devices travelling at sonic or supersonic speeds; and

(c) any act of terrorism that is not within the Terrorism Cover from time to time required to be taken out and maintained under this Contract.

Joint Names Policy: a policy of insurance which includes the Employer and the Contractor as composite insured and under which the insurers have no right of recourse against any person named as an insured, or, pursuant to clause 6·9, recognised as an insured thereunder.

Pool Re Cover: such insurance against loss or damage to work executed and Site Materials caused by or resulting from terrorism as is from time to time generally available from insurers who are members of the Pool Reinsurance Company Limited scheme or of any similar successor scheme.[52]

Specified Perils: fire, lightning, explosion, storm, flood, escape of water from any water tank, apparatus or pipe, earthquake, aircraft and other aerial devices or articles dropped therefrom, riot and civil commotion, but excluding Excepted Risks.

---

[51] In an All Risks Insurance policy for the Works, cover should not be reduced by any exclusion that goes beyond the terms of paragraph (b) in this definition; for example, an exclusion in terms that 'This Policy excludes all loss of or damage to the property insured due to defective design, plan, specification, materials or workmanship' would not be in accordance with the terms of the relevant Insurance Options or that definition. In relation to design defects, wider All Risks cover than that specified may be available to Contractors, though it is not standard.

[52] As respects Terrorism Cover and the requirements of Insurance Options A, B and C, see footnote [50] and the Intermediate Building Contract Guide.

continued 6·8

Terrorism Cover: Pool Re Cover or other insurance against loss or damage to work executed and Site Materials (and/or, for the purposes of clause 6·11·1, to an existing structure and/or its contents) caused by or resulting from terrorism.[52]

Sub-contractors – Specified Perils cover under Joint Names All Risks Policies

6·9   ·1   The Contractor, where Insurance Option A applies, and the Employer, where Insurance Option B or C applies, shall ensure that the Joint Names Policy referred to in paragraph A·1, A·3, B·1 or C·2 of Schedule 1 shall either:

     ·1   provide for recognition of each sub-contractor as an insured under the relevant Joint Names Policy; or

     ·2   include a waiver by the relevant insurers of any right of subrogation which they may have against any such sub-contractor

in respect of loss or damage by the Specified Perils to the Works or relevant Section, work executed and Site Materials and that this recognition or waiver shall continue up to and including the date of issue of any certificate or other document which states that in relation to the Works, the sub-contractor's works are practically complete or, if earlier, the date of termination of the sub-contractor's employment. Where there are Sections and the sub-contractor's works relate to more than one Section, the recognition or waiver for such sub-contractor shall nevertheless cease in relation to a Section upon the issue of such certificate or other document for his work in that Section.

   ·2   The provisions of clause 6·9·1 shall apply also in respect of any Joint Names Policy taken out by the Employer under paragraph A·2, or by the Contractor under paragraph B·2·1·2 or C·3·1·2 of Schedule 1.

   ·3   Where Insurance Option C applies, the Employer shall also ensure that the policy of insurance referred to in paragraph C·1 of Schedule 1 shall provide for recognition of any Named Sub-Contractor as an insured under that policy or include a waiver in respect of that Named Sub-Contractor in the terms referred to in clause 6·9·1·2, in either case up to and including the date of issue of such certificate or other document as is referred to in clause 6·9·1 or earlier date of termination of the Named Sub-Contractor's employment.

Terrorism Cover – policy extensions and premiums

6·10   ·1   To the extent that the Joint Names Policy for the Works and Site Materials excludes (or would otherwise exclude) loss or damage caused by terrorism, the Contractor, where Insurance Option A applies, or the Employer, where Insurance Option B or C applies, shall unless otherwise agreed take out and maintain, either as an extension to the Joint Names Policy or as a separate Joint Names Policy, in the same amount and for the required period of the Joint Names Policy, such Terrorism Cover as is specified in or by the Contract Particulars, subject to clauses 6·10·4 and 6·11.

   ·2   Where Insurance Option A applies and the Contractor is required to take out and maintain Pool Re Cover, the cost of that cover and its renewal shall be deemed to be included in the Contract Sum save that, if at any renewal of the cover there is a variation in the rate on which the premium is based, the Contract Sum shall be adjusted by the net amount of the difference between the premium paid by the Contractor and the premium that would have been paid but for the change in rate.

   ·3   Where Insurance Option A applies and Terrorism Cover other than Pool Re Cover is specified as required, the cost of such other cover and of its renewal shall be added to the Contract Sum.

   ·4   Where Insurance Option A applies and the Employer is a Local Authority, if at any renewal of the Terrorism Cover (of any type) there is an increase in the rate on which the premium is based, he may instruct the Contractor not to renew the Terrorism Cover. If he so instructs, the provisions of clauses 6·11·5·1 and 6·11·5·2 shall apply with effect from the renewal date.

Terrorism Cover – non-availability – Employer's options

6·11   ·1   If the insurers named in any Joint Names Policy notify either Party that, with effect from a specified date (the 'cessation date'), Terrorism Cover will cease and will no longer be available or will only continue to be available with a reduction in the scope or level of such cover, the recipient shall immediately notify the other Party.

continued 6·11

·2   The Employer, after receipt of such notification but before the cessation date, shall give notice to the Contractor either:

     ·1   that, notwithstanding the cessation or reduction in scope or level of Terrorism Cover, the Employer requires that the Works continue to be carried out; or

     ·2   that on the date stated in the Employer's notice (which shall be a date after the date of the insurers' notification but no later than the cessation date) the Contractor's employment under this Contract shall terminate.

·3   Where Insurance Option A applies and the Employer gives notice under clause 6·11·2·1 requiring continuation of the Works, he may instruct the Contractor to effect and maintain any alternative or additional form of Terrorism Cover then reasonably obtainable by the Contractor; the net additional cost to the Contractor of any such cover and its renewal shall be added to the Contract Sum.

·4   If the Employer gives notice of termination under clause 6·11·2·2, then upon and from such termination the provisions of clauses 8·12·2 to 8·12·5 (excluding clause 8·12·3·5) shall apply and, notwithstanding any other provision of this Contract, no further sum shall become due to the Contractor other than the amounts referred to in clauses 8·12·3·1 to 8·12·3·4.

·5   If the Employer does not give notice of termination under clause 6·11·2·2, then:

     ·1   if work executed and/or Site Materials suffer physical loss or damage caused by terrorism, the Contractor shall with due diligence restore the damaged work, replace or repair any lost or damaged Site Materials, remove and dispose of any debris and proceed with the carrying out of the Works;

     ·2   the restoration, replacement or repair of such loss or damage and (when required) the removal and disposal of debris shall be treated as a Variation, without deduction of retention and with no reduction in any amount payable to the Contractor pursuant to this clause 6·11·5·2 by reason of any act or neglect of the Contractor or of any sub-contractor which may have contributed to the physical loss or damage; and

     ·3   (where Insurance Option C applies) the requirement that the Works continue to be carried out shall not be affected by any loss or damage to the existing structures and/or their contents caused by terrorism but not so as thereby to impose any obligation on the Employer to reinstate the existing structures or affect the rights of either Party under paragraph C·4·4 of Schedule 1.

Joint Fire Code – compliance

Application of clauses

6·12   Clauses 6·13 to 6·15 apply where the Contract Particulars state that the Joint Fire Code applies.

Compliance with Joint Fire Code

6·13   The Parties shall comply with the Joint Fire Code and any amendments or revisions to it; the Employer shall ensure such compliance by all Employer's Persons and the Contractor shall ensure such compliance by all Contractor's Persons.

Breach of Joint Fire Code – Remedial Measures

6·14   ·1   If a breach of the Joint Fire Code occurs and the insurers under the Joint Names Policy in respect of the Works specify by notice to the Employer or the Contractor the remedial measures they require (the 'Remedial Measures'), the Party receiving the notice shall send copies of it to the other and to the Architect/Contract Administrator, and then:

     ·1   subject to clause 6·14·1·2, where the Remedial Measures relate to the obligation of the Contractor to carry out and complete the Works, the Contractor shall ensure that the Remedial Measures are carried out by such date as the insurers specify; and

     ·2   to the extent that the Remedial Measures require a Variation to the Works as described in the Contract Documents or in an Architect/Contract Administrator's instruction, the Architect/Contract Administrator shall issue such instructions as are necessary to enable compliance. If, in any emergency, compliance with the Remedial Measures in whole or in part requires the Contractor to supply materials or execute work before *continued 6·14·1·2* receiving instructions under this clause 6·14·1·2, the Contractor shall supply such limited materials and execute such limited work as are reasonably necessary to secure immediate compliance. The Contractor shall forthwith notify the Architect/Contract Administrator of the emergency and of the steps he is taking under this clause 6·14·1·2. Such work executed and materials supplied by the Contractor shall be treated as if they had been executed and supplied under an instruction requiring a Variation.

·2   If the Contractor, within 7 days of receipt of a notice specifying Remedial Measures not requiring an Architect/Contract Administrator's instruction under clause 6·14·1·2, does not begin to carry out or thereafter fails without reasonable cause regularly and diligently to proceed with the Remedial Measures, then the Employer may employ and pay other persons to carry out those Remedial Measures. The Contractor shall be liable for all additional costs incurred by the Employer in connection with such employment and an appropriate deduction shall be made from the Contract Sum.

Joint Fire Code – amendments/revisions

6·15   Where the Joint Fire Code is, under the Joint Names Policy, applicable to the Works and amendments or revisions are made to it after the Base Date, the cost, if any, of compliance by the Contractor with amendments or revisions made after that date shall be borne as stated in the Contract Particulars. If the cost is to be borne by the Employer, it shall be added to the Contract Sum.

Assignment

7·1   Neither the Employer nor the Contractor shall without the consent of the other assign this Contract or any rights thereunder.

Collateral Warranties

Notices

7·2   Each notice referred to in clauses 7·4 to 7·6 shall be given to the Contractor in accordance with clause 1·7·4.

Execution of Collateral Warranties

7·3   Where this Contract is executed as a deed, any collateral warranty to be entered into or procured pursuant to this section 7 shall be executed as a deed. Where this Contract is executed under hand, any such warranty may be executed under hand.

Contractor's Warranties – Purchasers and Tenants

7·4   In respect of any Purchasers and Tenants identified in Part 2 of the Contract Particulars, the Employer may by notice to the Contractor, identifying the Purchaser or Tenant and his interest in the Works, require that the Contractor within 14 days from receipt of that notice enter into with such Purchaser or Tenant a Collateral Warranty in the form CWa/P&T, completed in accordance with item (B) of Part 2 of the Contract Particulars.

Contractor's Warranty – Funder

7·5   In respect of a Funder identified in Part 2 of the Contract Particulars, the Employer may by notice to the Contractor require that the Contractor within 14 days from receipt of the Employer's notice enter into a Collateral Warranty with the Funder in the form CWa/F, completed in accordance with item (D) of Part 2 of the Contract Particulars.

Sub-Contractors' Warranties

7·6   Where Part 2 of the Contract Particulars provides for the giving by any sub-contractor of a Collateral Warranty to a Purchaser, Tenant or Funder or to the Employer, the Contractor shall within 21 days from receipt of the Employer's notice, identifying the relevant sub-contractor, type of warranty and beneficiary, comply with the Contract Documents as to obtaining such warranties in the form SCWa/P&T, SCWa/F or SCWa/E (as the case may be), completed in accordance with Part 2 of the Contract Particulars and subject to any amendments proposed by any such sub-contractor and approved by the Contractor and the Employer, such approval not to be unreasonably delayed or withheld.

General

Meaning of insolvency

8·1   For the purposes of these Conditions:

·1   a Party which is a company becomes Insolvent:

·1   when it enters administration within the meaning of Schedule B1 to the Insolvency Act 1986;

·2   on the appointment of an administrative receiver or a receiver or manager of its property under Chapter I of Part III of that Act, or the appointment of a receiver under Chapter II of that Part;

·3   on the passing of a resolution for voluntary winding-up without a declaration of solvency under section 89 of that Act; or

·4   on the making of a winding-up order under Part IV or V of that Act.

·2   a Party which is a partnership becomes Insolvent:

·1   on the making of a winding-up order against it under any provision of the Insolvency Act 1986 as applied by an order under section 420 of that Act; or

·2   when sequestration is awarded on the estate of the partnership under section 12 of the Bankruptcy (Scotland) Act 1985 or the partnership grants a trust deed for its creditors.

·3   a Party who is an individual becomes Insolvent:

·1   on the making of a bankruptcy order against him under Part IX of the Insolvency Act 1986; or

·2   on the sequestration of his estate under the Bankruptcy (Scotland) Act 1985 or when he grants a trust deed for his creditors.

·4   a Party also becomes Insolvent if:

·1   he enters into an arrangement, compromise or composition in satisfaction of his debts (excluding a scheme of arrangement as a solvent company for the purposes of amalgamation or reconstruction); or

·2   (in the case of a Party which is a partnership) each partner is the subject of an individual arrangement or any other event or proceedings referred to in this clause 8·1.

Each of clauses 8·1·1 to 8·1·4 also includes any analogous arrangement, event or proceedings in any other jurisdiction.

Notices under section 8

8·2   ·1   Notice of termination of the Contractor's employment shall not be given unreasonably or vexatiously.

·2   Such termination shall take effect on receipt of the relevant notice.

·3   Each notice referred to in this section shall be given in accordance with clause 1·7·4.

Other rights, reinstatement

8·3   ·1   The provisions of clauses 8·4 to 8·7 are without prejudice to any other rights and remedies of the Employer. The provisions of clauses 8·9 and 8·10 and (in the case of termination under either of those clauses) the provisions of clause 8·12, are without prejudice to any other rights and remedies of the Contractor.

     ·2   Irrespective of the grounds of termination, the Contractor's employment may at any time be reinstated if and on such terms as the Parties agree.

Termination by Employer

Default by Contractor

8·4   ·1   If, before practical completion of the Works, the Contractor:

        ·1   without reasonable cause wholly or substantially suspends the carrying out of the Works; or

        ·2   fails to proceed regularly and diligently with the Works; or

        ·3   refuses or neglects to comply with a notice or instruction from the Architect/Contract Administrator requiring him to remove any work, materials or goods not in accordance with this Contract and by such refusal or neglect the Works are materially affected; or

        ·4   fails to comply with clause 3·5, 3·7 or 7·1; or

        ·5   fails to comply with clause 3·18,

        the Architect/Contract Administrator may give to the Contractor a notice specifying the default or defaults (the 'specified default or defaults').

     ·2   If the Contractor continues a specified default for 14 days from receipt of the notice under clause 8·4·1, the Employer may on, or within 21 days from, the expiry of that 14 day period by a further notice to the Contractor terminate the Contractor's employment under this Contract.

     ·3   If the Employer does not give the further notice referred to in clause 8·4·2 (whether as a result of the ending of any specified default or otherwise) but the Contractor repeats a specified default (whether previously repeated or not), then, upon or within a reasonable time after such repetition, the Employer may by notice to the Contractor terminate that employment.

Insolvency of Contractor

8·5   ·1   If the Contractor is Insolvent, the Employer may at any time by notice to the Contractor terminate the Contractor's employment under this Contract.

     ·2   The Contractor shall immediately notify the Employer if he makes any proposal, gives notice of any meeting or becomes the subject of any proceedings or appointment relating to any of the matters referred to in clause 8·1.

     ·3   As from the date the Contractor becomes Insolvent, whether or not the Employer has given such notice of termination:

        ·1   clauses 8·7·3 to 8·7·5 and (if relevant) clause 8·8 shall apply as if such notice had been given;

        ·2   the Contractor's obligations under Article 1 and these Conditions to carry out and complete the Works shall be suspended; and

        ·3   the Employer may take reasonable measures to ensure that the site, the Works and Site Materials are adequately protected and that such Site Materials are retained on site; the Contractor shall allow and shall not hinder or delay the taking of those measures.

Corruption

8·6   The Employer shall be entitled by notice to the Contractor to terminate the Contractor's employment under this or any other contract with the Employer if, in relation to this or any other such contract, the Contractor or any person employed by him or acting on his behalf shall have committed an offence under the Bribery Act 2010, or, where the Employer is a Local Authority, shall have given any fee or reward the receipt of which is an offence under sub-section (2) of section 117 of the Local Government Act 1972.

Consequences of termination under clauses 8·4 to 8·6

8·7   If the Contractor's employment is terminated under clause 8·4, 8·5 or 8·6:

   ·1   the Employer may employ and pay other persons to carry out and complete the Works and to make good any defects of the kind referred to in clause 2·30, and he and they may enter upon and take possession of the site and the Works and (subject to obtaining any necessary third party consents) may use all temporary buildings, plant, tools, equipment and Site Materials for those purposes;

   ·2   the Contractor shall:

      ·1   when required in writing by the Architect/Contract Administrator to do so (but not before), remove or procure the removal from the Works of any temporary buildings, plant, tools, equipment, goods and materials belonging to the Contractor or Contractor's Persons;

      ·2   if so required by the Employer (or by the Architect/Contract Administrator on his behalf) within 14 days of the date of termination, assign (so far as assignable and so far as he may lawfully be required to do so) to the Employer, without charge, the benefit of any agreement for the supply of materials or goods and/or for the execution of any work for the purposes of this Contract[53];

   ·3   no further sum shall become due to the Contractor under this Contract other than any amount that may become due to him under clause 8·7·5 or 8·8·2 and the Employer need not pay any sum that has already become due either:

      ·1   insofar as the Employer has given or gives a Pay Less Notice under clause 4·11·5; or

      ·2   if the Contractor, after the last date upon which such notice could have been given by the Employer in respect of that sum, has become insolvent within the meaning of clauses 8·1·1 to 8·1·3;

   ·4   following the completion of the Works and the making good of defects in them (or of instructions otherwise, as referred to in clause 2·30), an account of the following shall within 3 months thereafter be set out in a certificate issued by the Architect/Contract Administrator or a statement prepared by the Employer:

      ·1   the amount of expenses properly incurred by the Employer, including those incurred pursuant to clause 8·7·1 and, where applicable, clause 8·5·3·3, and of any direct loss and/or damage caused to the Employer and for which the Contractor is liable, whether arising as a result of the termination or otherwise;

      ·2   the amount of payments made to the Contractor; and

      ·3   the total amount which would have been payable for the Works in accordance with this Contract;

   ·5   if the sum of the amounts stated under clauses 8·7·4·1 and 8·7·4·2 exceeds the amount stated under clause 8·7·4·3, the difference shall be a debt payable by the Contractor to the Employer or, if that sum is less, by the Employer to the Contractor.

---

[53]   Clause 8·7·2·2 may not be effectual in cases of Contractor's insolvency.

Employer's decision not to complete the Works

8·8   ·1   If within the period of 6 months from the date of termination of the Contractor's employment the Employer decides not to have the Works carried out and completed, he shall forthwith notify the Contractor. Within a reasonable time from the date of such notification, or if no notification is given but within that 6 month period the Employer does not commence to make arrangements for such carrying out and completion, then within 2 months of the expiry of that 6 month period, the Employer shall send to the Contractor a statement setting out:

       ·1   the total value of work properly executed at the date of termination or date on which the Contractor became Insolvent, ascertained in accordance with these Conditions as if that employment had not been terminated, together with any amounts due to the Contractor under these Conditions not included in such total value; and

       ·2   the aggregate amount of any expenses properly incurred by the Employer and of any direct loss and/or damage caused to the Employer and for which the Contractor is liable, whether arising as a result of the termination or otherwise.

   ·2   After taking into account amounts previously paid to the Contractor under this Contract, if the amount stated under clause 8·8·1·2 exceeds the amount stated under clause 8·8·1·1, the difference shall be a debt payable by the Contractor to the Employer or, if the clause 8·8·1·2 amount is less, by the Employer to the Contractor.

Termination by Contractor

Default by Employer

8·9   ·1   If the Employer:

       ·1   does not pay by the final date for payment the amount due to the Contractor in accordance with clause 4·11 and/or any VAT properly chargeable on that amount; or

       ·2   interferes with or obstructs the issue of any certificate due under this Contract; or

       ·3   fails to comply with clause 7·1; or

       ·4   fails to comply with clause 3·18,

the Contractor may give to the Employer a notice specifying the default or defaults (the 'specified default or defaults').

   ·2   If before practical completion of the Works the carrying out of the whole or substantially the whole of the uncompleted Works is suspended for a continuous period of the length stated in the Contract Particulars by reason of:

       ·1   Architect/Contract Administrator's instructions under clause 2·13, 3·11 or 3·12; and/or

       ·2   any impediment, prevention or default, whether by act or omission, by the Employer, the Architect/Contract Administrator, the Quantity Surveyor or any of the Employer's Persons

(but in either case excluding such instructions as are referred to in clause 8·11·1·2), then, unless in either case that is caused by the negligence or default of the Contractor or of any of the Contractor's Persons, the Contractor may give to the Employer a notice specifying the event or events (the 'specified suspension event or events').

   ·3   If a specified default or a specified suspension event continues for 14 days from the receipt of notice under clause 8·9·1 or 8·9·2, the Contractor may on, or within 21 days from, the expiry of that 14 day period by a further notice to the Employer terminate the Contractor's employment under this Contract.

   ·4   If the Contractor for any reason does not give the further notice referred to in clause 8·9·3, but (whether previously repeated or not):

       ·1   the Employer repeats a specified default; or

       ·2   a specified suspension event is repeated for any period, such that the regular progress of the Works is or is likely to be materially affected thereby, *continued 8·9·4* then, upon or within a reasonable time after such repetition, the Contractor may by notice to the Employer terminate the Contractor's employment under this Contract.

Insolvency of Employer

8·10 ·1 If the Employer is Insolvent, the Contractor may by notice to the Employer terminate the Contractor's employment under this Contract;

·2 the Employer shall immediately notify the Contractor if he makes any proposal, gives notice of any meeting or becomes the subject of any proceedings or appointment relating to any of the matters referred to in clause 8·1;

·3 as from the date the Employer becomes Insolvent, the Contractor's obligations under Article 1 and these Conditions to carry out and complete the Works shall be suspended.

Termination by either Party

8·11 ·1 If, before practical completion of the Works, the carrying out of the whole or substantially the whole of the uncompleted Works is suspended for the relevant continuous period of the length stated in the Contract Particulars by reason of one or more of the following events:

·1 force majeure;

·2 Architect/Contract Administrator's instructions under clause 2·13, 3·11 or 3·12 issued as a result of the negligence or default of any Statutory Undertaker;

·3 loss or damage to the Works occasioned by any of the Specified Perils;

·4 civil commotion or the use or threat of terrorism and/or the activities of the relevant authorities in dealing with such event or threat; or

·5 the exercise by the United Kingdom Government of any statutory power which directly affects the execution of the Works,

then either Party, subject to clause 8·11·2, may upon the expiry of that relevant period of suspension give notice to the other that, unless the suspension ceases within 7 days after the date of receipt of that notice, he may terminate the Contractor's employment under this Contract. Failing such cessation within that 7 day period, he may then by further notice terminate that employment.

·2 The Contractor shall not be entitled to give notice under clause 8·11·1 in respect of the matter referred to in clause 8·11·1·3 where the loss or damage to the Works occasioned by a Specified Peril was caused by the negligence or default of the Contractor or of any of the Contractor's Persons.

Consequences of Termination under clauses 8·9 to 8·11, etc.

8·12 If the Contractor's employment is terminated under any of clauses 8·9 to 8·11, under clause 6·11·2·2 or under paragraph C·4·4 of Schedule 1:

·1 no further sums shall become due to the Contractor otherwise than in accordance with this clause 8·12;

·2 the Contractor shall with all reasonable dispatch remove or procure the removal from the site of any temporary buildings, plant, tools and equipment belonging to the Contractor and Contractor's Persons and, subject to the provisions of clause 8·12·5, all goods and materials (including Site Materials);

·3 where the Contractor's employment is terminated under clause 8·9 or 8·10, the Contractor shall as soon as reasonably practicable prepare and submit an account or, where terminated under clause 8·11 or 6·11·2·2 or under paragraph C·4·4 of Schedule 1, the Contractor shall at the Employer's option either prepare and submit that account or, not later than 2 months after the date of termination, provide the Employer with all documents necessary for the Employer to do so, which the Employer shall do with reasonable dispatch (and in any event within 3 months of receipt of such documents). The account shall set out the amounts referred to in clauses 8·12·3·1 to 8·12·3·4 and, if applicable, clause 8·12·3·5, namely:

continued 8·12·3

·1 the total value of work properly executed at the date of termination of the Contractor's employment, ascertained in accordance with these Conditions as if the employment had not been terminated, together with any other amounts due to the Contractor under these Conditions;

·2 any sums ascertained in respect of direct loss and/or expense under clause 4·17 (whether ascertained before or after the date of termination);

·3 the reasonable cost of removal under clause 8·12·2;

·4 the cost of materials or goods (including Site Materials) properly ordered for the Works for which the Contractor then has paid or is legally bound to pay;

·5 any direct loss and/or damage caused to the Contractor by the termination;

·4 the account shall include the amount, if any, referred to in clause 8·12·3·5 only where the Contractor's employment is terminated either:

·1 under clause 8·9 or 8·10; or

·2 under clause 8·11·1·3, if the loss or damage to the Works occasioned by any of the Specified Perils was caused by the negligence or default of the Employer or of any of the Employer's Persons;

·5 after taking into account amounts previously paid to the Contractor under this Contract, the Employer shall pay to the Contractor (or vice versa) the amount properly due in respect of the account within 28 days of its submission to the other Party, without deduction of any retention. Payment by the Employer for any such materials and goods as are referred to in clause 8·12·3·4 shall be subject to such materials and goods thereupon becoming the Employer's property.

Mediation

9·1   Subject to Article 7, if a dispute or difference arises under this Contract which cannot be resolved by direct negotiations, each Party shall give serious consideration to any request by the other to refer the matter to mediation.[54]

Adjudication

9·2   If a dispute or difference arises under this Contract which either Party wishes to refer to adjudication, the Scheme shall apply, subject to the following:

    ·1   for the purposes of the Scheme the Adjudicator shall be the person (if any) and the nominating body shall be that stated in the Contract Particulars;

    ·2   where the dispute or difference is or includes a dispute or difference relating to clause 3·15 and as to whether an instruction issued thereunder is reasonable in all the circumstances:

       ·1   the Adjudicator to decide such dispute or difference shall (where practicable) be an individual with appropriate expertise and experience in the specialist area or discipline relevant to the instruction or issue in dispute;

       ·2   if the Adjudicator does not have the appropriate expertise and experience, the Adjudicator shall appoint an independent expert with such expertise and experience to advise and report in writing on whether or not the instruction under clause 3·15 is reasonable in all the circumstances.

Arbitration

Conduct of arbitration

9·3   Any arbitration pursuant to Article 8 shall be conducted in accordance with the JCT 2011 edition of the Construction Industry Model Arbitration Rules (CIMAR), provided that if any amendments to that edition of the Rules have been issued by the JCT the Parties may, by a joint notice in writing to the Arbitrator, state that they wish the arbitration to be conducted in accordance with the Rules as so amended. References in clause 9·4 to a Rule or Rules are references to such Rule(s) as set out in the JCT 2011 edition of CIMAR.[55]

Notice of reference to arbitration

9·4   ·1   Where pursuant to Article 8 either Party requires a dispute or difference to be referred to arbitration, that Party shall serve on the other Party a notice of arbitration to such effect in accordance with Rule 2.1 identifying the dispute and requiring the other Party to agree to the appointment of an arbitrator. The Arbitrator shall be an individual agreed by the Parties or, failing such agreement within 14 days (or any agreed extension of that period) after the notice of arbitration is served, appointed on the application of either Party in accordance with Rule 2.3 by the person named in the Contract Particulars.

    ·2   Where two or more related arbitral proceedings in respect of the Works fall under separate arbitration agreements, Rules 2.6, 2.7 and 2.8 shall apply.

---

[54]   See the Intermediate Building Contract Guide.

[55]   Arbitration or legal proceedings are **not** an appeal against the decision of the Adjudicator but are a consideration of the dispute or difference as if no decision had been made by an Adjudicator.

continued 9·4

·3   After an arbitrator has been appointed either Party may give a further notice of arbitration to the other Party and to the Arbitrator referring any other dispute which falls under Article 8 to be decided in the arbitral proceedings and Rule 3.3 shall apply.

Powers of Arbitrator

9·5   Subject to the provisions of Article 8 and clause 1·9, the Arbitrator shall, without prejudice to the generality of his powers, have power to rectify this Contract so that it accurately reflects the true agreement made by the Parties, to direct such measurements and/or valuations as may in his opinion be desirable in order to determine the rights of the Parties and to ascertain and award any sum which ought to have been the subject of or included in any certificate and to open up, review and revise any certificate, opinion, decision, requirement or notice and to determine all matters in dispute which shall be submitted to him in the same manner as if no such certificate, opinion, decision, requirement or notice had been given.

Effect of award

9·6   Subject to clause 9·7 the award of the Arbitrator shall be final and binding on the Parties.

Appeal – questions of law

9·7   The Parties hereby agree pursuant to section 45(2)(a) and section 69(2)(a) of the Arbitration Act 1996 that either Party may (upon notice to the other Party and to the Arbitrator):

·1   apply to the courts to determine any question of law arising in the course of the reference; and

·2   appeal to the courts on any question of law arising out of an award made in an arbitration under this arbitration agreement.

Arbitration Act 1996

9·8   The provisions of the Arbitration Act 1996 shall apply to any arbitration under this Contract wherever the same, or any part of it, shall be conducted.

Schedules

Schedule 1   Insurance Options

(Clause 6·7)

Insurance Option A

(New Buildings – All Risks Insurance of the Works by the Contractor)[56]

Contractor to take out and maintain a Joint Names Policy

A·1   The Contractor shall take out and maintain with insurers approved by the Employer a Joint Names Policy for All Risks Insurance with cover no less than that specified in clause 6·8[57] for the full reinstatement value of the Works or (where applicable) Sections (plus the percentage, if any, stated in the Contract Particulars to cover professional fees)[58] and (subject to clause 2·28) shall maintain such Joint Names Policy up to and including the date of issue of the Practical Completion Certificate or, if earlier, the date of termination of the Contractor's employment (whether or not the validity of that termination is contested).

The obligation to maintain the Joint Names Policy shall not apply in relation to a Section after the date of issue of the Section Completion Certificate for that Section.

Insurance documents – failure by Contractor to insure

A·2   The Contractor shall send to the Architect/Contract Administrator for deposit with the Employer the Joint Names Policy referred to in paragraph A·1, each premium receipt for it and any relevant endorsements of it. If the Contractor defaults in taking out or in maintaining the Joint Names Policy as required by paragraph A·1 (or fails to maintain a policy in accordance with paragraph A·3), the Employer may himself take out and maintain a Joint Names Policy against any risk in respect of which the default has occurred and the amount paid or payable by him in respect of premiums may be deducted by him from any sums due or to become due to the Contractor under this Contract or shall be recoverable from the Contractor as a debt.

Use of Contractor's annual policy – as alternative

A·3   If and so long as the Contractor independently of this Contract maintains an insurance policy which in respect of the Works or Sections:

---

[56]   **Insurance Option A** is applicable to the erection of new buildings where the **Contractor** is required to take out a Joint Names Policy for All Risks Insurance of the Works and **Insurance Option B** is applicable where the **Employer** has elected to take out that Joint Names Policy. **Insurance Option C** is for use in the case of alterations of or extensions to existing structures; under it, the **Employer** is required to take out a Joint Names Policy for All Risks Insurance for the Works and also a Joint Names Policy to insure the existing structures and their contents owned by him or for which he is responsible against loss or damage by the Specified Perils. Some Employers (e.g. tenants and homeowners) may not be able readily to obtain the Joint Names cover, in particular that under paragraph C·1. If so, Option C should not be stated to apply and consequential amendments may be necessary. See the Intermediate Building Contract Guide.

[57]   The risks and costs that All Risks Insurance is required to cover are defined by exclusions. Policies issued by insurers are not standardised; the way in which insurance for these risks is expressed varies and **in some cases it may not be possible for insurance to be taken out against certain of the risks required to be covered.** In the case of Terrorism Cover, where the extension of cover will involve an additional premium and may in certain situations be difficult to effect, the requirement is now expressly limited to Pool Re Cover or such other cover as is agreed and set out in the Contract Particulars. That extension and any other relevant details require discussion and agreement between the Parties and their insurance advisers **prior to entering into the Contract.** See the Intermediate Building Contract Guide.

[58]   As to reinstatement value, irrecoverable VAT and other costs, see the Intermediate Building Contract Guide. As respects sub-contractors, note also the provisions of clause 6·9.

continued A·3

·1   provides (inter alia) All Risks Insurance with cover and in amounts no less than those specified in paragraph A·1; and

·2   is a Joint Names Policy,

such policy shall satisfy the Contractor's obligations under paragraph A·1. The Employer may at any reasonable time inspect the policy and premium receipts for it or require that they be sent to the Architect/Contract Administrator for such inspection. So long as the Contractor, as and when reasonably required to do so, supplies the documentary evidence that the policy is being so maintained, the Contractor shall not be obliged under paragraph A·2 to deposit the policy and premium receipts with the Employer. The annual renewal date of the policy, as supplied by the Contractor, is stated in the Contract Particulars.

Loss or damage, insurance claims and Contractor's obligations

A·4   ·1   If loss or damage affecting any executed work or Site Materials is occasioned by any risk covered by the Joint Names Policy, then, upon its occurrence or later discovery, the Contractor shall forthwith give notice both to the Architect/Contract Administrator and to the Employer of its extent, nature and location.

      ·2   Subject to clause 6·11·5·2 and paragraph A·4·4, the occurrence of such loss or damage shall be disregarded in computing any amounts payable to the Contractor under this Contract.

      ·3   After any inspection required by the insurers in respect of a claim under the Joint Names Policy has been completed, the Contractor shall with due diligence restore the damaged work, replace or repair any lost or damaged Site Materials, remove and dispose of any debris and proceed with the carrying out and completion of the Works.

      ·4   The Contractor, for himself and for all his sub-contractors who pursuant to clause 6·9 are recognised as an insured under the Joint Names Policy, shall authorise the insurers to pay all monies from such insurance to the Employer. The Employer shall pay all such amounts to the Contractor (without deduction of retention and less only the amount stated in paragraph A·4·5) by instalments under Architect/Contract Administrator's certificates issued on the dates fixed for the issue of Interim Certificates.

      ·5   The Employer may retain from the monies paid by the insurers the amount properly incurred by the Employer in respect of professional fees up to an amount which shall not exceed the amount of the additional percentage cover for those fees or (if less) the amount paid by insurers in respect of those fees.

      ·6   In respect of the restoration, replacement or repair of such loss or damage and (when required) the removal and disposal of debris, the Contractor shall not be entitled to any payment other than amounts received under the Joint Names Policy or payable to him under clause 6·11·5·2, where applicable.

Insurance Option B

(New Buildings – All Risks Insurance of the Works by the Employer)[56]

Employer to take out and maintain a Joint Names Policy

B·1   The Employer shall take out and maintain a Joint Names Policy for All Risks Insurance with cover no less than that specified in clause 6·8[57] for the full reinstatement value of the Works or (where applicable) Sections (plus the percentage, if any, stated in the Contract Particulars to cover professional fees)[58] and (subject to clause 2·28) shall maintain such Joint Names Policy up to and including the date of issue of the Practical Completion Certificate or, if earlier, the date of termination of the Contractor's employment (whether or not the validity of that termination is contested).

The obligation to maintain the Joint Names Policy shall not apply in relation to a Section after the date of issue of the Section Completion Certificate for that Section.

Evidence of Insurance

B·2   ·1   Except where the Employer is a Local Authority:

·1   the Employer shall, as and when reasonably required by the Contractor, produce documentary evidence and receipts showing that the Joint Names Policy has been taken out and is being maintained; and

·2   if the Employer defaults in taking out or in maintaining the Joint Names Policy, the Contractor may himself take out and maintain a Joint Names Policy against any risk in respect of which the default has occurred and the amount paid or payable by him in respect of the premiums shall be added to the Contract Sum.

·2   Where the Employer is a Local Authority, the Employer shall, as and when reasonably required by the Contractor, produce to the Contractor a copy of the cover certificate issued by the insurer named in the Joint Names Policy certifying that Terrorism Cover is being provided under that policy.

Loss or damage, insurance claims, Contractor's obligations and payment by Employer

B·3   ·1   If loss or damage affecting any executed work or Site Materials is occasioned by any risk covered by the Joint Names Policy, then, upon its occurrence or later discovery, the Contractor shall forthwith give notice both to the Architect/Contract Administrator and to the Employer of its extent, nature and location.

·2   Subject to clause 6·11·5·2 and paragraph B·3·5, the occurrence of such loss or damage shall be disregarded in computing any amounts payable to the Contractor under this Contract.

·3   After any inspection required by the insurers in respect of a claim under the Joint Names Policy has been completed, the Contractor shall with due diligence restore the damaged work, replace or repair any lost or damaged Site Materials, remove and dispose of any debris and proceed with the carrying out and completion of the Works.

·4   The Contractor, for himself and for all his sub-contractors who pursuant to clause 6·9 are recognised as an insured under the Joint Names Policy, shall authorise the insurers to pay all monies from such insurance to the Employer.

·5   The restoration, replacement or repair of such loss or damage and (when required) the removal and disposal of debris shall be treated as a Variation.

Insurance Option C

(Insurance by the Employer of Existing Structures and Works in or Extensions to them)[56]

Existing structures and contents – Joint Names Policy for Specified Perils

C·1   The Employer shall take out and maintain a Joint Names Policy in respect of the existing structures (which from the Relevant Date shall include any Relevant Part to which clause 2·25 refers) together with the contents thereof owned by him or for which he is responsible, for the full cost of reinstatement[58], repair or replacement of loss or damage due to any of the Specified Perils up to and including the date of issue of the Practical Completion Certificate or last Section Completion Certificate, or (if earlier) the date of termination of the Contractor's employment (whether or not the validity of that termination is contested). The Contractor shall authorise the insurers to pay all monies from such insurance to the Employer.

The Works – Joint Names Policy for All Risks

C·2   The Employer shall take out and maintain a Joint Names Policy for All Risks Insurance with cover no less than that specified in clause 6·8[57] for the full reinstatement value of the Works or (where applicable) Sections (plus the percentage, if any, stated in the Contract Particulars to cover professional fees)[58] and (subject to clause 2·28) shall maintain such Joint Names Policy up to and including the date of issue of the Practical Completion Certificate or, if earlier, the date of termination of the Contractor's employment (whether or not the validity of that termination is contested).

The obligation to maintain the Joint Names Policy under this paragraph C·2 shall not apply in relation to any Section after the date of issue of the Section Completion Certificate for that Section.

Evidence of Insurance

C·3   ·1   Except where the Employer is a Local Authority:

        ·1   the Employer shall, as and when reasonably required by the Contractor, produce documentary evidence and receipts showing that the Joint Names Policies required under paragraphs C·1 and C·2 have been taken out and are being maintained;

        ·2   if the Employer defaults in taking out or in maintaining either of those Joint Names Policies, the Contractor may himself take out and maintain a Joint Names Policy against any risk in respect of which the default has occurred and for that purpose, in relation to any default under paragraph C·1, shall have such right of entry and inspection as may be required to make a survey and inventory of the existing structures and the relevant contents; and

        ·3   in the event of any such default, a sum equivalent to the premiums paid or payable by the Contractor pursuant to paragraph C·3·1·2 shall be added to the Contract Sum.

    ·2   Where the Employer is a Local Authority, the Employer shall, as and when reasonably required by the Contractor, produce to the Contractor copies of the cover certificates issued by the insurers named in the Joint Names Policies under paragraphs C·1 and C·2 which certify that Terrorism Cover is being provided under each policy.

Loss or damage – insurance claims and Contractor's obligations

C·4   ·1   If during the carrying out of the Works there is any loss of or damage of any kind to any of the existing structures or their contents and/or if loss or damage affecting any executed work or Site Materials is occasioned by any of the risks covered by the Joint Names Policy referred to in paragraph C·2 or C·3 then, upon its occurrence or later discovery, the Contractor shall forthwith give notice both to the Architect/Contract Administrator and to the Employer of its extent, nature and location.

    ·2   Subject to clause 6·11·5·2 and paragraph C·4·5·2, the occurrence of such loss or damage to executed work or Site Materials shall be disregarded in computing any amounts payable to the Contractor under this Contract.

    ·3   The Contractor, for himself and for all his sub-contractors who pursuant to clause 6·9 are recognised as an insured under the Joint Names Policy referred to in paragraph C·2, shall authorise the insurers to pay all monies from the insurances referred to in paragraphs C·2 and C·3 to the Employer.

continued C·4

·4   If there is material loss of or damage to any of the existing structures and it is just and equitable, the Contractor's employment under this Contract may within 28 days of the occurrence of such loss or damage be terminated at the option of either Party by notice given to the other in accordance with clause 1·7·4. If such notice is given:

    ·1   either Party may within 7 days of receiving such a notice (but not thereafter) invoke the dispute resolution procedures that apply under this Contract in order that it may be decided whether the termination is just and equitable; and

    ·2   upon the giving of such notice of termination or, where those dispute resolution procedures have been invoked, upon any final upholding of the notice of termination, the provisions of clauses 8·12·2 to 8·12·5 (except clause 8·12·3·5) shall apply.

·5   If no notice of termination is served under paragraph C·4·4, or if the notice of termination is disputed and is not upheld, then:

    ·1   after any inspection required by the insurers under the Joint Names Policy referred to in paragraph C·2 has been completed, the Contractor shall with due diligence restore the damaged work, replace or repair any lost or damaged Site Materials, remove and dispose of any debris and proceed with the carrying out and completion of the Works; and

    ·2   the restoration, replacement or repair of such loss or damage and (when required) the removal and disposal of debris shall be treated as a Variation.

Schedule 2   Named Sub-Contractors

(Clause 3·7)

1   The Contractor shall notify the Architect/Contract Administrator of the date on which he enters into the sub-contract with the Named Sub-Contractor.

2   If the Contractor is unable to enter into a sub-contract in accordance with clause 3·7 and the particulars given in the Contract Documents, he shall immediately notify the Architect/Contract Administrator, specifying which of the particulars prevent the execution of the sub-contract. If the Architect/Contract Administrator is reasonably satisfied that the specified particulars have prevented execution, he shall issue an instruction which may:

    ·1   change the particulars so as to remove the impediment to execution; or

    ·2   omit the work; or

    ·3   omit the work from the Contract Documents and substitute a provisional sum.

3   An instruction under paragraph 2·1 or 2·2 shall be regarded as an instruction under clause 3·11 requiring a Variation and shall be valued under clause 5·2 and the provisions of clauses 2·19 *(Adjustment of Completion Date)* and 4·17 *(Loss and Expense)* shall as relevant apply. Where the instruction is under paragraph 2·2 the Employer may, subject to the terms of clause 2·7, have the omitted work executed in accordance with that clause. An instruction under paragraph 2·3 shall be dealt with in accordance with paragraph 5.

4   At any time prior to the Contractor entering into a sub-contract in accordance with clause 3·7 the Architect/Contract Administrator may issue an instruction that the work is to be carried out by a person other than the person named in the Contract Bills/Specification/Work Schedules. Such instruction shall omit the work from the Contract Documents and substitute a provisional sum which shall be dealt with in accordance with paragraph 5.

5   ·1   In an instruction as to the expenditure of a provisional sum under clause 3·13 the Architect/Contract Administrator may require work to be executed by a person named in the instruction, who shall then be employed by the Contractor as a Named Sub-Contractor.

    ·2   Any such instruction shall incorporate a description of the work and all particulars of the tender of the named person for that work in an Intermediate Named Sub-Contract Invitation to Tender and Tender (ICSub/NAM/IT and ICSub/NAM/T) as completed, together with the Tender Documents referred to therein.

    ·3   Unless the Contractor makes reasonable objection to entering into a sub-contract with the named person within 14 days of the date of issue of the instruction, he shall enter into a sub-contract with him for the execution of the work, using the Intermediate Named Sub-Contract Agreement (ICSub/NAM/A) and incorporating the Named Sub-Contract Conditions.

6   The Contractor shall not terminate a Named Sub-Contractor's employment otherwise than under clause 7·4, 7·5 or 7·6 of the Named Sub-Contract Conditions, nor without the prior consent of the Architect/Contract Administrator accept termination or repudiation of the sub-contract by the Named Sub-Contractor, such consent not to be unreasonably delayed or withheld. In either case the Contractor shall notify the Architect/Contract Administrator as soon as is reasonably practicable of any events likely to lead to termination of the Named Sub-Contractor's employment, however arising.

7   Whether or not the notification referred to in paragraph 6 has been given, if the Named Sub-Contractor's employment terminates before completion of the sub-contract work, the Contractor shall notify the Architect/Contract Administrator, giving particulars of the circumstances. The Architect/Contract Administrator shall issue instructions as may be necessary in which he shall:

    ·1   name another person to execute the work, or the outstanding balance of it, in accordance with paragraph 5·2 and subject to paragraph 5·3; or

    ·2   instruct the Contractor to make his own arrangements for the execution of the work or the outstanding balance of the work, in which case the Contractor may sub-contract the work in accordance with clause 3·5; or

continued 7

·3   omit the work or the outstanding balance of work.

8   Where an instruction is issued under paragraph 7 in respect of a Named Sub-Contractor who was named in the Contract Bills/Specification/Work Schedules and whose employment has been terminated either under clause 7·4, 7·5 or 7·6 of the Named Sub-Contract Conditions or with the Architect/Contract Administrator's consent:

·1   an instruction under paragraph 7·1 shall be regarded as a Relevant Event for the purposes of clause 2·19 *(Adjustment of Completion Date)*, but not as a Relevant Matter for the purposes of clause 4·17 *(Loss and Expense)*, and the Contract Sum shall be adjusted by the amount of the increase or the reduction in the price of the second Named Sub-Contractor for the work not carried out by the first Named Sub-Contractor when compared with the first Named Sub-Contractor's price for that work. In that adjustment there shall be excluded from the price of the second Named Sub-Contractor any amount included for the repair of defects in the work of the first Named Sub-Contractor;

·2   an instruction under paragraph 7·2 or 7·3 shall be regarded as one requiring a Variation to be valued under clause 5·2 and both as a Relevant Event for the purposes of clause 2·19 and a Relevant Matter for the purposes of clause 4·17.

Where the instruction is under paragraph 7·3 the Employer may, subject to the terms of clause 2·7, have the omitted work executed in accordance with that clause.

9   Where an instruction is issued under paragraph 7 in respect of a Named Sub-Contractor who was named in an instruction as to the expenditure of a Provisional Sum under paragraph 5 and whose employment has been terminated under clause 7·4, 7·5 or 7·6 of the Named Sub-Contract Conditions or with the Architect/Contract Administrator's consent, such instruction shall be regarded as a further instruction issued in relation to the Provisional Sum.

10   ·1   Where the employment of a Named Sub-Contractor is terminated otherwise than under clause 7·4, 7·5 or 7·6 of the Named Sub-Contract Conditions and without the Architect/Contract Administrator's consent, the provisions of paragraph 8·1, 8·2 or 9 (as appropriate) shall apply in respect of the instructions under paragraph 7, but only to the extent that they result in a reduction in the Contract Sum and the instruction shall not be regarded as a Relevant Event or Relevant Matter for the purposes of clauses 2·19 and 4·17.

·2   Where the Named Sub-Contractor's employment is terminated under clause 7·4, 7·5 or 7·6 of the Named Sub-Contract Conditions or with the Architect/Contract Administrator's consent:

·1   the Contractor shall take such reasonable action as is necessary to recover from the Named Sub-Contractor, whether under clause 7·7 of the Named Sub-Contract Conditions or otherwise, any additional amounts payable to the Contractor by the Employer as a result of the application of paragraph 8·1, 8·2 or 9 together with an amount equal to any liquidated damages that would have been payable or allowable by the Contractor to the Employer under clause 2·23 but for the application of any of those paragraphs;

·2   the Contractor shall account to the Employer for any amounts so recovered;

·3   in taking such action the Contractor shall not be required to invoke the dispute resolution procedures under the sub-contract unless the Employer shall have agreed to indemnify the Contractor against any legal costs reasonably incurred in relation thereto;

·4   if the Contractor fails to comply with this paragraph 10·2 he shall repay to the Employer any additional amounts paid as a result of the application of paragraph 8·1, 8·2 or 9 and shall pay or allow an amount equal to the liquidated damages referred to in paragraph 10·2·1.

11   ·1   Whether or not a Named Sub-Contractor is responsible to the Employer for exercising reasonable care and skill in:

·1   the design of the sub-contract works insofar as they have been or are to be designed by the Named Sub-Contractor;

·2   the selection of the kinds of materials and goods for the sub-contract works insofar as such materials and goods have been or will be selected by him; or

continued 11·1

·3   the satisfaction of any performance specification or requirement relating to the sub-contract works,

the Contractor shall not be responsible to the Employer under this Contract for anything to which such terms relate, nor, through the Contractor, shall the Named Sub-Contractor be so responsible; provided that this shall not be construed as affecting the obligations of the Contractor or any sub-contractor in regard to the supply of goods, materials and workmanship.

·2   The provisions of paragraph 11·1 shall apply notwithstanding that the Sub-Contract Sum stated in Article 2 of the Intermediate Named Sub-Contract Agreement referred to in clause 3·7 or paragraph 5·3 included for the supply of any design, selection or satisfaction as referred to in paragraph 11·1, and that such Sub-Contract Sum is included within the Contract Sum or the Contract Sum as finally adjusted.

12   Clause 3·7 and this Schedule shall not apply to the execution of any part of the Works by a Statutory Undertaker executing work solely in that capacity.

13   Save as expressly stated in this Schedule, the Contractor shall remain wholly responsible for carrying out and completing the Works in all respects in accordance with clause 2·1 notwithstanding the naming of a Named Sub-Contractor for the execution of any such work.

Schedule 3   Forms of Bonds

(Clauses 4·6 and 4·9)

(Agreed between the JCT and the British Bankers' Association)

Part 1: Advance Payment Bond[59]

1   THE parties to this Bond are:

_____

whose registered office is at _____

_____ ('the Surety'), and

_____

of _____

_____ ('the Employer').

2   The Employer and _____ ('the Contractor')

have agreed to enter into a contract ('the Contract') for building works ('the Works') at _____

_____

3   The Employer has agreed to pay the Contractor the sum of [_____]
as an advance payment of sums due to the Contractor under the Contract ('the Advance Payment')
for reimbursement by the Surety on the following terms:

    ·1   when the Surety receives a demand from the Employer in accordance with clause 3·2 below
the Surety shall repay the Employer the sum demanded up to the amount of the Advance
Payment;

    ·2   the Employer shall in making any demand provide to the Surety a completed notice of demand
in the form of the **Schedule** attached hereto which shall be accepted as conclusive evidence
for all purposes under this Bond. The signatures on any such demand must be authenticated
by the Employer's bankers;

    ·3   the Surety shall within 5 Business Days after receiving the demand pay to the Employer the
sum so demanded. 'Business Day' means the day (other than a Saturday or a Sunday) on
which commercial banks are open for business in London.

4   Payments due under this Bond shall be made notwithstanding any dispute between the Employer
and the Contractor and whether or not the Employer and the Contractor are or might be under any
liability one to the other. Payment by the Surety under this Bond shall be deemed a valid payment for
all purposes of this Bond and shall discharge the Surety from liability to the extent of such payment.

---

[59]   Not applicable where the Employer is a Local Authority.

5   The Surety consents and agrees that the following actions by the Employer may be made and done without notice to or consent of the Surety and without in any way affecting changing or releasing the Surety from its obligations under this Bond and the liability of the Surety hereunder shall not in any way be affected hereby. The actions are:

    ·1   waiver by the Employer of any of the terms, provisions, conditions, obligations and agreements of the Contractor or any failure to make demand upon or take action against the Contractor;

    ·2   any modification or changes to the Contract; and/or

    ·3   the granting of any extensions of time to the Contractor without affecting the terms of clause 7·3 below.

6   The Surety's maximum aggregate liability under this Bond which shall commence on payment of the Advance Payment by the Employer to the Contractor shall be the amount of [_____] which sum shall be reduced by the amount of any reimbursement made by the Contractor to the Employer as advised by the Employer in writing to the Surety.

7   The obligations of the Surety under this Bond shall cease upon whichever is the earliest of:

    ·1   the date on which the Advance Payment is reduced to nil as certified in writing to the Surety by the Employer;

    ·2   the date on which the Advance Payment or any balance thereof is repaid to the Employer by the Contractor (as certified in writing to the Surety by the Employer) or by the Surety; and

    ·3   [*longstop date to be given*],

    and any claims hereunder must be received by the Surety in writing on or before such earliest date.

8   This Bond is not transferable or assignable without the prior written consent of the Surety. Such written consent will not be unreasonably withheld.

9   Notwithstanding any other provisions of this Bond nothing in this Bond confers or is intended to confer any right to enforce any of its terms on any person who is not a party to it.

10   This Bond shall be governed and construed in accordance with the laws of England and Wales.

IN WITNESS whereof this Deed of Guarantee has been duly executed and delivered on the date below:

Signed as a Deed by: _____

    as the Attorney and on behalf of the Surety: _____

In the presence of:

_____
witness' signature

_____
witness' name

_____
witness' address

_____

Date: _____

Schedule to Advance Payment Bond

(clause 3·2 of the Bond)

Notice of Demand

Date of Notice: _____

Date of Bond: _____

Employer: _____

Surety: _____

The Bond has come into effect.

We hereby demand payment of the sum of

£ _____ (amount in words)
which does not exceed the amount of reimbursement for which the Contractor is in default at the date
of this notice.

Address for payment: _____

_____

This Notice is signed by the following persons who are authorised by the Employer to act for and on
his behalf:

Signed by _____

      Name: _____

      Official Position: _____

Signed by _____

      Name: _____

      Official Position: _____

The above signatures to be authenticated by the Employer's bankers

Part 2: Bond in respect of payment for off-site materials and/or goods

1 THE parties to this Bond are:

_____

whose registered office is at _____

_____ ('the Surety'), and

_____

of _____

_____ ('the Employer').

2 The Employer and _____ ('the Contractor')

have agreed to enter into a contract ('the Contract') for building works ('the Works') at _____

_____

3 Subject to the relevant provisions of the Contract as summarised below but with which the Surety shall not at all be concerned:

·1 the Employer has agreed to include the amount stated as due in Interim Certificates (as defined in the Contract) for payment by the Employer the value of those materials or goods or items pre-fabricated for inclusion in the Works listed by the Employer in a list which has been included as part of the Contract ('the Listed Items'), before their delivery to or adjacent to the Works; and

·2 the Contractor has agreed to insure the Listed Items against loss or damage for their full value under a policy of insurance protecting the interests of the Employer and the Contractor during the period commencing with the transfer of the property in the items to the Contractor until they are delivered to or adjacent to the Works; and

·3 this Bond shall exclusively relate to the amount paid to the Contractor in respect of the Listed Items which have not been delivered to or adjacent to the Works.

4 The Employer shall in making any demand provide to the Surety a Notice of Demand in the form of the **Schedule** attached hereto which shall be accepted as conclusive evidence for all purposes under this Bond. The signatures on any such demand must be authenticated by the Employer's bankers.

5 The Surety shall within 5 Business Days after receiving the demand pay to the Employer the sum so demanded. 'Business Day' means the day (other than a Saturday or a Sunday) on which commercial banks are open for business in London.

6 Payments due under this Bond shall be made notwithstanding any dispute between the Employer and the Contractor and whether or not the Employer and the Contractor are or might be under any liability one to the other. Payment by the Surety under this Bond shall be deemed a valid payment for all purposes of this Bond and shall discharge the Surety from liability to the extent of such payment.

7 The Surety consents and agrees that the following actions by the Employer may be made and done without notice to or consent of the Surety and without in any way affecting changing or releasing the Surety from its obligations under this Bond and the liability of the Surety hereunder shall not in any way be affected hereby. The actions are:

·1 waiver by the Employer of any of the terms, provisions, conditions, obligations and agreements of the Contractor or any failure to make demand upon or take action against the Contractor;

continued 7

·2   any modification or changes to the Contract; and/or

·3   the granting of an extension of time to the Contractor without affecting the terms of clause 9·2 below.

8   The Surety's maximum aggregate liability under this Bond shall be *[_____].

9   The obligations of the Surety under this Bond shall cease upon whichever is the earlier of:

·1   the date on which all the Listed Items have been delivered to or adjacent to the Works as certified in writing to the Surety by the Employer; or

·2   [*longstop date to be given*],

and any claims hereunder must be received by the Surety in writing on or before such earlier date.

10   The Bond is not transferable or assignable without the prior written consent of the Surety. Such written consent will not be unreasonably withheld.

11   Notwithstanding any other provisions of this Bond nothing in this Bond confers or is intended to confer any right to enforce any of its terms on any person who is not a party to it.

12   This Bond shall be governed and construed in accordance with the laws of England and Wales.

*The value stated in the Contract which the Employer considers will be sufficient to cover him for maximum payments to the Contractor for the Listed Items that will have been made and not delivered to the site at any one time.

IN WITNESS whereof this Deed of Guarantee has been duly executed and delivered on the date below:

Signed as a Deed by: _____

as the Attorney and on behalf of the Surety: _____

In the presence of:

_____
witness' signature

_____
witness' name

_____
witness' address

_____

Date: _____

Schedule to Bond

(clause 4 of the Bond)

Notice of Demand

Date of Notice: _____

Date of Bond: _____

Employer: _____

Surety: _____

We hereby demand payment of the sum of £_____
being the amount stated as due in respect of Listed Items included in the amount stated as due in an
Interim Certificate(s) for payment which has been duly made to the Contractor by the Employer but
such Listed Items have not been delivered to or adjacent to the Works.

Address for payment: _____

_____

This Notice is signed by the following persons who are authorised by the Employer to act for and on
his behalf:

Signed by _____

      Name: _____

      Official Position: _____

Signed by _____

      Name: _____

      Official Position: _____

The above signatures to be authenticated by the Employer's bankers

Deemed calculation of Contract Sum – labour

1   The Contract Sum shall be deemed to have been calculated in the manner set out below and shall be subject to adjustment in the events specified hereunder.

·1   The Contract Sum is based upon the types and rates of contribution, levy and tax payable by a person in his capacity as an employer and which at the Base Date are payable by the Contractor. A type and a rate so payable are in paragraph 1·2 referred to as a 'tender type' and a 'tender rate'.

·2   If any of the tender rates other than a rate of levy payable by virtue of the Industrial Training Act 1982 is increased or decreased, or if a tender type ceases to be payable, or if a new type of contribution, levy or tax which is payable by a person in his capacity as an employer becomes payable after the Base Date, then in any such case the net amount of the difference between what the Contractor actually pays or will pay in respect of:

·1   workpeople engaged upon or in connection with the Works either on or adjacent to the site; and

·2   workpeople directly employed by the Contractor who are engaged upon the production of materials or goods for use in or in connection with the Works and who operate neither on nor adjacent to the site and to the extent that they are so engaged

or because of his employment of such workpeople and what he would have paid had the alteration, cessation or new type of contribution, levy or tax not become effective shall, as the case may be, be paid to or allowed by the Contractor.

·3   There shall be added to the net amount paid to or allowed by the Contractor under paragraph 1·2, in respect of each person employed by the Contractor who is engaged upon or in connection with the Works either on or adjacent to the site and who is not within the definition of workpeople in paragraph 11·3, the same amount as is payable or allowable in respect of a craftsman under paragraph 1·2 or such proportion of that amount as reflects the time (measured in whole working days) that each such person is so employed.

·4   For the purposes of paragraph 1·3:

·1   no period of less than 2 whole working days in any week shall be taken into account and periods of less than a whole working day shall not be aggregated to amount to a whole working day;

·2   "the same amount as is payable or allowable in respect of a craftsman" shall refer to the amount in respect of a craftsman employed by the Contractor (or by any domestic sub-contractor under a sub-contract to which paragraph 3 refers) under the rules or decisions or agreements of the Construction Industry Joint Council or other wage-fixing body and, where those rules or decisions or agreements provide for more than one rate of wage, emolument or other expense for a craftsman, shall refer to the amount in respect of a craftsman employed as aforesaid to whom the highest rate is applicable; and

·3   "employed by the Contractor" shall mean an employment to which the Income Tax (Pay As You Earn) Regulations 2003 apply.

·5   The Contract Sum is based upon the types and rates of refund of the contributions, levies and taxes payable by a person in his capacity as an employer and upon the types and rates of premium receivable by a person in his capacity as an employer being in each case types and rates which at the Base Date are receivable by the Contractor. Such a type and such a rate are in paragraph 1·6 referred to as a 'tender type' and a 'tender rate'.

·6   If any of the tender rates is increased or decreased or if a tender type ceases to be payable or if a new type of refund of any contribution, levy or tax payable by a person in his capacity as an employer becomes receivable or if a new type of premium receivable by a person in his capacity as an employer becomes receivable after the Base Date, then in any such case the net amount of the difference between what the Contractor actually receives or will receive in respect of workpeople as referred to in paragraphs 1·2·1 and 1·2·2 or because of his employment of such workpeople and what he would have received had the alteration, cessation or new type of refund or premium not become effective shall, as the case may be, be paid to or allowed by the Contractor.

·7   The references in paragraphs 1·5 and 1·6 to premiums shall be construed as meaning all payments howsoever they are described which are made under or by virtue of an Act of Parliament to a person in his capacity as an employer and which affect the cost to an employer of having persons in his employment.

·8   Where employer's contributions are payable by the Contractor in respect of workpeople as referred to in paragraphs 1·2·1 and 1·2·2 whose employment is contracted-out employment within the meaning of the Pension Schemes Act 1993, the Contractor shall for the purpose of recovery or allowance under this paragraph 1 be deemed to pay employer's contributions as if that employment were not contracted-out employment.

·9   The references in paragraph 1 to contributions, levies and taxes shall be construed as meaning all impositions payable by a person in his capacity as an employer howsoever they are described and whoever the recipient which are imposed under or by virtue of an Act of Parliament and which affect the cost to an employer of having persons in his employment.

Deemed calculation of Contract Sum – materials

2   The Contract Sum shall be deemed to have been calculated in the manner set out below and shall be subject to adjustment in the events specified hereunder.

·1   The Contract Sum is based upon the types and rates of duty, if any, and tax, if any (other than any VAT which is treated, or is capable of being treated, as input tax by the Contractor), by whomsoever payable which at the Base Date are payable on the import, purchase, sale, appropriation, processing, use or disposal of the materials, goods, electricity, fuels, materials taken from the site as waste or any other solid, liquid or gas necessary for the execution of the Works by virtue of any Act of Parliament. A type and a rate so payable are in paragraph 2·2 referred to as a 'tender type' and a 'tender rate'.

·2   If, in relation to any materials or goods or any electricity or fuels or materials taken from the site as waste or any other solid, liquid or gas necessary for the execution of the Works including temporary site installations for those Works, a tender rate is increased or decreased or a tender type ceases to be payable or a new type of duty or tax (other than any VAT which is treated, or is capable of being treated, as input tax by the Contractor) becomes payable on the import, purchase, sale, appropriation, processing, use or disposal of any of the above things after the Base Date, then in any such case the net amount of the difference between what the Contractor actually pays in respect of those materials, goods, electricity, fuels, materials taken from the site as waste or any other solid, liquid or gas and what he would have paid in respect of them had the alteration, cessation or imposition not occurred shall, as the case may be, be paid to or allowed by the Contractor. In this paragraph 2·2 "a new type of duty or tax" includes an additional duty or tax and a duty or tax imposed in regard to any of the above in respect of which no duty or tax whatever was previously payable (other than any VAT which is treated, or is capable of being treated, as input tax by the Contractor).

Sub-contract work – incorporation of provisions to like effect

3   ·1   If the Contractor sub-contracts any portion of the Works to a sub-contractor other than a Named Sub-Contractor he shall incorporate in the sub-contract provisions to the like effect as the provisions of this Fluctuations Option (excluding this paragraph 3) including the percentage stated in the Contract Particulars pursuant to paragraph 12 which are applicable for the purposes of this Contract.

·2   If the price payable under such a sub-contract as referred to in paragraph 3·1 is increased above or decreased below the price in such sub-contract by reason of the operation of the said incorporated provisions, then the net amount of such increase or decrease shall, as the case may be, be paid to or allowed by the Contractor under this Contract.

Notification by Contractor

4   ·1   The Contractor shall notify the Architect/Contract Administrator of the occurrence of any of the events referred to in such of the following provisions as are applicable for the purposes of this Contract:

      ·1   paragraph 1·2;

      ·2   paragraph 1·6;

      ·3   paragraph 2·2;

      ·4   paragraph 3·2.

  ·2   Any notification required to be given under paragraph 4·1 shall be given within a reasonable time after the occurrence of the event to which it relates, and notification in that time shall be a condition precedent to any payment being made to the Contractor in respect of the event in question.

Agreement – Quantity Surveyor and Contractor

5   The Quantity Surveyor and the Contractor may agree what shall be deemed for all the purposes of this Contract to be the net amount payable to or allowable by the Contractor in respect of the occurrence of any event such as is referred to in any of the provisions listed in paragraph 4·1.

Fluctuations added to or deducted from Contract Sum

6   Any amount which from time to time becomes payable to or allowable by the Contractor by virtue of paragraphs 1 and 2 or paragraph 3 shall, as the case may be, be added to or deducted from:

  ·1   the Contract Sum; and

  ·2   any amounts payable to the Contractor and which are calculated in accordance with clause 8·12·3·1.

The addition or deduction to which this paragraph 6 refers shall be subject to the provisions of paragraphs 7 to 9·1.

Evidence and computations by Contractor

7   As soon as is reasonably practicable the Contractor shall provide such evidence and computations as the Architect/Contract Administrator or the Quantity Surveyor may reasonably require to enable the amount payable to or allowable by the Contractor by virtue of paragraphs 1 and 2 or paragraph 3 to be ascertained; and in the case of amounts payable to or allowable by the Contractor under paragraph 1·3 (or paragraph 3 for amounts payable to or allowable under the provisions in the sub-contract to the like effect as paragraphs 1·3 and 1·4) – employees other than workpeople – such evidence shall include a certificate signed by or on behalf of the Contractor each week certifying the validity of the evidence reasonably required to ascertain such amounts.

No alteration to Contractor's profit

8   No addition to or deduction from the Contract Sum made by virtue of paragraph 6 shall alter in any way the amount of profit of the Contractor included in that Sum.

Position where Contractor in default over completion

9   ·1   Subject to the provisions of paragraph 9·2 no amount shall be added or deducted in the computation of the amount stated as due in an Interim Certificate or in the Final Certificate in respect of amounts otherwise payable to or allowable by the Contractor by virtue of paragraphs 1 and 2 or paragraph 3 if the event (as referred to in the provisions listed in paragraph 4·1) in respect of which the payment or allowance would be made occurs after the Completion Date.

  ·2   Paragraph 9·1 shall not be applied unless:

      ·1   the printed text of clauses 2·19 and 2·20 is unamended and forms part of the Conditions; and

continued 9·2

·2   the Architect/Contract Administrator has, in respect of every notification by the Contractor under clause 2·19, notified the Contractor of the extension of time, if any, that he considers to be in accordance with that clause.

Work etc. to which paragraphs 1 to 3 not applicable

10   Paragraphs 1 to 3 shall not apply in respect of:

·1   work for which the Contractor is allowed daywork rates under clause 5·4;

·2   work executed by any named person as a sub-contractor under clause 3·7 (fluctuations in relation to such sub-contractors shall be dealt with under any provision in relation thereto which may be included in the appropriate sub-contract);

·3   changes in the rate of VAT charged on the supply of goods or services by the Contractor to the Employer under this Contract.

Definitions

11   In this Fluctuations Option:

·1   the Base Date means the date stated as such in the Contract Particulars;

·2   "materials" and "goods" include timber used in formwork but do not include other consumable stores, plant and machinery;

·3   "workpeople" means persons whose rates of wages and other emoluments (including holiday credits) are governed by the rules or decisions or agreements of the Construction Industry Joint Council or some other wage-fixing body for trades associated with the building industry;

·4   "wage-fixing body" means a body which lays down recognised terms and conditions of workers;

·5   "recognised terms and conditions" means terms and conditions of workers in comparable employment in the trade or industry, or section of trade or industry, in which the employer in question is engaged which have been settled by an agreement or award to which the parties are employers' associations and independent trade unions which represent (generally, or in the district in question, as the case may be) a substantial proportion of the employers and of the workers in the trade, industry or section being workers of the description to which the agreement or award relates.

Percentage addition to fluctuation payments or allowances

12   There shall be added to the amount paid to or allowed by the Contractor under:

·1   paragraph 1·2,

·2   paragraph 1·3,

·3   paragraph 1·6,

·4   paragraph 2·2

the percentage stated in the Contract Particulars.

Each provision applies unless otherwise stated in the Contract Particulars.

Collaborative working

1   The Parties shall work with each other and with other project team members in a co-operative and collaborative manner, in good faith and in a spirit of trust and respect. To that end, each shall support collaborative behaviour and address behaviour which is not collaborative.

Health and safety

2   ·1   Without limiting either Party's statutory and/or regulatory duties and responsibilities and/or the specific health and safety requirements of this Contract, the Parties will endeavour to establish and maintain a culture and working environment in which health and safety is of paramount concern to everybody involved with the project.

    ·2   In addition to the specific health and safety requirements of this Contract, the Contractor undertakes to:

       ·1   comply with any and all approved codes of practice produced or promulgated by the Health and Safety Executive and/or the Health and Safety Commission;

       ·2   ensure that all personnel engaged by the Contractor and members of the Contractor's supply chain on site receive appropriate site-specific health and safety induction training and regular refresher training;

       ·3   ensure that all such personnel have access at all times to competent health and safety advice in accordance with regulation 7 of the Management of Health and Safety at Work Regulations 1999; and

       ·4   ensure that there is full and proper health and safety consultation with all such personnel in accordance with the Health and Safety (Consultation with Employees) Regulations 1996.

Cost savings and value improvements

3   ·1   The Contractor is encouraged to propose changes to designs and specifications for the Works and/or to the programme for their execution that may benefit the Employer, whether in the form of a reduction in the cost of the Works or their associated life cycle costs, through practical completion at a date earlier than the Completion Date or otherwise.

    ·2   The Contractor shall provide details of his proposed changes, identifying them as suggested under this paragraph 3, together with his assessment of the benefit he believes the Employer may obtain, expressed in financial terms, and a quotation.

    ·3   Where the Employer wishes to implement a change proposed by the Contractor, the Parties shall negotiate with a view to agreeing its value, the financial benefit and any adjustment to the Completion Date. Upon agreement, the change and the amount of any adjustment of the Contract Sum shall be confirmed in an Architect/Contract Administrator's instruction, together with the share of the financial benefit to be paid to the Contractor and any adjustment to the Completion Date.

    ·4   Original proposals by the Contractor under this paragraph 3 may only be instructed in accordance with it, provided always that nothing shall prevent the Employer from utilising other contractors to implement such changes after practical completion of the Works.

Sustainable development and environmental considerations

4   ·1   The Contractor is encouraged to suggest economically viable amendments to the Works which, if instructed as a Variation, may result in an improvement in environmental performance in the carrying out of the Works or of the completed Works.

continued 4

·2   The Contractor shall provide to the Employer all information that he reasonably requests regarding the environmental impact of the supply and use of materials and goods which the Contractor selects.

Performance Indicators and monitoring

5   ·1   The Employer shall monitor and assess the Contractor's performance by reference to any performance indicators stated or identified in the Contract Documents.

    ·2   The Contractor shall provide to the Employer all information that he may reasonably require to monitor and assess the Contractor's performance against the targets for those performance indicators.

    ·3   Where the Employer considers that a target for any of those performance indicators may not be met, he may inform the Contractor who shall submit his proposals for improving his performance against that target to the Employer.

Notification and negotiation of disputes

6   With a view to avoidance or early resolution of disputes or differences (subject to Article 7), each Party shall promptly notify the other of any matter that appears likely to give rise to a dispute or difference. The senior executives nominated in the Contract Particulars (or if either is not available, a colleague of similar standing) shall meet as soon as practicable for direct, good faith negotiations to resolve the matter.